A Journey of Ascent Towards the

A Journ
Toward   ͻoom

By Hͻ   ͼnes

Unless otherwise indicated all scripture quotations are from the New Kings James Version®[NKJV], Copyright©1982 by Thomas Nelson. Used by permission. All rights reserved.

NET Scripture quotations marked [NET] are from the NET Bible® copyright ©1996, 2019 by Biblical Studies Press, L.L.C. http://netbible.com. Used by permission. All rights reserved.

ESV Scripture quotations marked [ESV] are from the ESV® Bible (The Holy Bible, English Standard Version®), copyright © 2001 by Crossway Bibles, a publishing ministry of Good News Publishers. Used by permission. All rights reserved.

LEB Scripture quotations marked [LEB] are from the Lexham English Bible. Copyright 2010 Logos Bible Software. Lexham is a registered trademark of Logos Bible Software.

NIV scripture quotations marked [NIV] are from NIV THE HOLY BIBLE, NEW INTERNATIONAL VERSION®, NIV® Copyright © 1973, 1978, 1984, 2011 by Biblica, Inc.™ Used by permission. All rights reserved worldwide.

For general information on our other work, products and services or to obtain technical support, please make contact via www.call2come.org. The Author publishes books in a variety of electronic and print formats. Some content that appears in print may not be available in electronic books, and vice versa.

Cover Design: Mike Pike

ISBN: Print 978-1-9196224-8-4

First published in July 2022.

Second Edition September 2022

For more information and resources and to contact the Author, please go to www.call2come.org.

The Spirit and the Bride say Come

Revelation 22:17 [ESV]

A Journey of Ascent Towards the Bridegroom

Howard Barnes
Call2Come

A Journey of Ascent Towards the Bridegroom

Table of Contents

In Appreciation 10

About the Author 12

Endorsements 13

Part 1: The Journey through the Foothills. 16

Chapter 1: Introduction – A Tale in Two Halves 17

Chapter 2: From Birth to Rebirth 21

Chapter 3: School Daze 31

Chapter 4: University and the Student life 37

Chapter 5: Lord, There Must be More? 52

Chapter 6: A Marriage Made in Heaven 64

Chapter 7: The Call to Cornwall 76

Chapter 8: Brass Band Music is the Music of Heaven 82

Chapter 9: Success and the Self-Made Man 93

Chapter 10: Time Travel 105

Chapter 11: The Secret Chamber and Seeking His Face ... 110

Chapter 12: Called and Chosen for Mission 117

Chapter 13: Learning by Observation and Revelation 132

Part 2: The Journey Upwards and Onwards 147

Chapter 14: A Meeting at the Well 148

Chapter 15: The Wake-Up Call 155

Chapter 16: Understanding the Times and Seasons 166

Chapter 17: Marriage, the Bride and the Bridegroom as the Central Themes of Scripture 178

Chapter 18: The Apostolic and Prophetic Mantle................184

Chapter 19: The Revelation of the Bride and God's Eternal Purpose...194

Chapter 20: Jesus Gets Engaged to be Married, Another Bridal Revelation..200

Chapter 21: 'Fast' Tracking 208

Chapter 22: By Royal Appointment Divine Connections.......217

Chapter 23: Our Heavenly Father is the Chief Strategist – The Shofar Vision...227

Chapter 24: The Authority of the Bride 233

Chapter 25: Bridal Authority at the Gate 241

Chapter 26: The Revelation of the Eternal Nature of the Bride 246

Chapter 27: Exercising Bridal Authority in Intercession and by Proclamation and Decree 253

Chapter 28: Lest we forget Israel; The Bride is the One New Man 259

Chapter 29: The Call2Come Core Message – Even so, Come Lord Jesus 271

Chapter 30: Preparing Ourselves as His Bride 282

Chapter 31: Understanding this World Pandemic as a Time of Bridal Preparation...293

Conclusion 303

A Message from Co-Director of the Call2Come Ministry – Mike Pike..**305**

About Call2Come **309**

Find Out More **311**

In Appreciation

I am humbled by the measure of encouragement and support I have received in writing this book. Firstly I want to thank the Lord Jesus for His insistence and persistence over many years from the very first time He told me that one day I would write it. When that time had fully come, He gave me the grace to do so in just four weeks and reminded me of so much that had been forgotten about the journey I endured. Though the completed first draft took only a few weeks, I appreciate the friends who commented, edited, or proofread the manuscript in the early stages.

I am so grateful in particular to Philip Thomas and Philip Clarke, long-time university friends who were the first to review and begin editing the script. Also to Benson Nyangor (Kenya), Akemi Yoko (Japan), Rev David Munby (retired UK) for his guidance in editorial, theological, and biblical matters, and Jill Munby, David's wife, who helped with the final proofreading. David and Jill are both special friends of my wife Tricia and me.

Of course, this book, though partly autobiographical, is indeed about myself and my close friend and co-director Mike Pike. Thank you so much Mike for your encouragement and for embarking on this journey with me.

Finally, many thanks to you, Tricia, for your patience with me and prayers for me, and your great love. I would not have had the experiences that are described in this book, without your willingness to let me leave you at home alone for weeks at a time as I went on missions abroad. Also bless you for tolerating the hours alone spent recently whilst I was editing and preparing it for publication. Thank you Tricia for always being there.

About the Author

Howard Barnes was born in Newcastle Under Lyme, England in 1944 to Salvation Army pastor parents. His relationship with Jesus as his Saviour began as an eight-year-old boy. It was a very real experience for him. After Secondary Education, he studied Theology at Chester College and subsequently became a Secondary School teacher serving as the Head of Divinity in several London Schools. After moving to Cornwall, England he also served as the youth leader and as part of the leadership team of the Falmouth Baptist Church and later of a new Community Church plant. In 2003 he retired from teaching, after 37 years, to full-time serve the Lord as a missionary to the nations, operating under an apostolic mantle.

He now co-directs a ministry called Call2Come International with Dr Michael Pike. It is a ministry that is deeply passionate about two things 1.) the worldwide Church discovery of the meaning of real unity and fulfil the prayer of Jesus in John 17:21 & 23, *"that they may be One even as we are One"* and 2) to see the Body of Christ understand and embrace its end-time identity as His precious Bride and to prepare her for the return of Jesus. It is a deep longing of his heart to hear the Bride cry, in unison with the Holy Spirit, Come Lord Jesus Come and to experience that alignment when both, "the Spirit and the Bride say Come!"

Call2Come's mission is to Awaken, Prepare and Protect the Bride so that she is, "without spot or blemish", "a pure virgin" and ready for Her marriage to Her Bridegroom King.

Endorsements

It is a pleasure to write this double commendation for Howard's book. Howard and I have known each other for many years, yet in reading his personal story I found myself drawn in by links I was not previously aware of. I know you will be drawn in too by his warm-hearted narrative of God's goodness. Then we come to the second half of Howard's book, and the reason for my double commendation. It reveals Howard's passion. It will come as no surprise that he is passionate about the Church as the Bride of Christ. He is, however, also supremely passionate about Christ as the Bridegroom. This book will inspire us all to be equally passionate as we work together in readiness for Christ's return. It is within this passion that we will discover the true beauty of God's redemptive plan. Thank you Howard for your ministry, and for your faithfulness in serving God's kingdom far and wide.

Dr Hugh Osgood. Free Churches President of Churches Together in England. Co-Chair of the UK Charismatic and Pentecostal Leaders' Conference. Founding President of Churches in Communities International.

Reading this book is like finding a chest, it may look quite ordinary but open the lid and you are dazzled by the treasures inside. Here are nuggets of pure gold, diamonds, emeralds and pearls. Let me share a few; firstly the words of the Lord Jesus given to the author;

"Anointing is having My power and My presence within you – preach it and I'll bring conviction.

13

Teach it and I'll bring revelation.

Command it and I'll do it."

There are so many more treasures; read it, meditate on it. It can change your life for, "We are transitioning from seeing Jesus as our Saviour to seeing Him as the Bridegroom and ourselves as His precious bride." In embracing this identity, "we will be driven by a passionate love for Jesus and an intense desire for intimacy with Him as our Bridegroom King."

Read it and be transformed.

Catherine Jinadu. Wife of the General Overseer New Covenant Church, Founder of Liberty making people free.

Howard encourages us to look at the Lord's goodness in our own lives with thankfulness. I loved reading his interesting journey into faith. There are unexpected surprises and lives changed in wonderful ways including here in the UK! God gives us hope for our own backyard. I especially felt the strong call of the book to come up higher and know the Lord's love more deeply. There is always more!

Bob Bain. Director of Welcome Network UK. bobbain@hotmail.co.uk

This is a very timely book, as it is the time prophetically for the Bride to make herself ready. The Lord raised Call2come to underline this Divine purpose, and to keep in focus the ultimate eternal glory of the Church, to be the Bride for God's Beloved Son.

What an incentive to keep first love a priority and to be watching for the coming of the Bridegroom! Dovetail Shalom Ministries heartily endorse this book and know your heart will be blessed as you read.

Brenda Taylor. Dovetail Shalom Ministries UK

Part 1: The Journey through the Foothills.

Chapter 1: Introduction – A Tale in Two Halves

Revelation 4:1 "Come up here, and I will show you what must take place after this."

Revelation 21: 9 "Come, I will show you the bride, the wife of the Lamb."

Song of Songs 2:10 "My lover said to me, "Rise up, my darling! Come away with me, my fair one!"

Genesis 24:58 "So they called Rebekah and asked her, "Will you go with this man?" And she said, "I will go."

This story is about my journey in understanding that Jesus is not only our Saviour but is also our Bridegroom King and we therefore, a part of His precious corporate Bride. It is also an account of how the ministry known as 'Call2Come International' came into existence and although written in an autobiographical style it also contains the beautiful message about the Bride and the revelation of the Bridal Paradigm.

The whole of our Christian journey is a continuous journey, a climb or ascent, a tough mountain climb which demands much determination and not a little pain if we are to reach our destination. But they say that without pain there is no gain and without any test there is no testimony. This story certainly is a testimony to His love and grace!

This is a story in two parts:

Part 1: A Journey through the Foothills

Part 2: The Journey of Ascent Upwards and Onwards

Our Christian journey is not along a smooth and level path but one that has many valleys and hills, troughs and peaks to surmount. The Spirit of God is always calling us onward and asking us to 'Come up higher".

Some might suggest that this book is really two books not one: an autobiography and another book about the Bridal Paradigm but I would disagree. Part 1 is indeed about my own life up until I met with Mike Pike who was to be a co-director of the ministry with me, but more importantly it is about the lessons I learned on my journey since these provide the foundation for Part 2.

All those experiences narrated in the first part are to do with learning about His ways through experiencing His acts. It was these lessons that God used to prepare me for the revelations about the Bride that he was going to share with Mike and myself, some of which are described in the second part. I hope that Part 2 in particular will help you to understand your own true end-time identity as His precious Bride.

The Father through the Spirit is always inviting us to "Come up a little higher". But He knows that to do so we have to leave behind so much that is of the earth if we want to reach the place where we can see what He sees and step into the realms of spiritual realities where He dwells. It is a place where that 'oneness' with the Father that Jesus prayed for in John 17 is experienced and where His mind and ours, His heart and ours, His plans and ours, converge as one; And we are then able to partner with Him in fulfilling His glorious eternal purposes. Nothing gives Him more pleasure than this and nothing gives us such a sense of wholeness, of worth and fulfilment.

However, the greatest revelation that anyone can receive is to know that God has reserved, for those who believe, a place at the Wedding of the Lamb where the Bridegroom and the Bride are the key characters. Yet more precious still, is the fact that our attendance at that wedding is not just as a spectator but as His very own Bride. Since this wedding closes the mortal chapter of Church history, our life here on earth is all about our personal preparation for this royal wedding and in order to prepare for it we must ascend. We must climb up "a little higher". But many sadly don't understand nor desire to.

Even though many identify as a believer, they live their Christian life on a very earthly plain and only occasionally grasp things from a heavenly perspective. God the Father wants us to see things from His vantage point and that's from the point of view of Jesus, His Son, being the Bridegroom. That's why the Spirit is repeatedly calling us to "Come up a little higher". And we can go higher only because Christ came lower and took upon Himself the form of a man in order to suffer death on the cross for us; making a way for our righteous Father to forgive us our sins and adopt us into His forever family.

Now the Holy Spirit has Himself in our generation also come lower, even to roam the earth looking for a bride for the Father's Son. He wants to take us all on a journey to meet our Bridegroom but we have to be willing to go. And that journey is an ascent in the Spirit upwards and onwards. The Spirit is calling us and we have to recognise that call and answer the eternal question just as Rebekah did and the Shulamite woman did. "Will you go with this man?", "Will you come away with me?"

Chapter 2: From Birth to Rebirth

My earliest memory, strange as it may seem, was of lying on my back as a young child, in a Victorian-style coach pram, gazing up at the moving clouds and making raspberry sounds with my lips as babies do. I was born to be a brass player. That must have been very early on, just a few years after my birth on 19th January 1944 in Newcastle under Lyme, in Staffordshire, England, towards the end of the Second World War.

Early on in their married life and before I was born, both my parents felt a very strong call to the mission field and were prepared to go as Officers in charge of the Salvation Army School in Harare, Zimbabwe. However, World War II was raging all over Europe. Passenger ships were not sailing as German U-boats patrolled the seas. Air tickets were unavailable too since the skies were too dangerous. They prayerfully waited for things to change but finally resigned themselves to serving God in the UK. However they promised the Father that if ever He gifted them with a son then they would call him Howard after Commissioner Howard, the territorial Commissioner of Rhodesia which now is called Zimbabwe of course, and perhaps he would one day go and serve God in Africa.

I remembered this when years later I set out on my first foreign missionary trip to Uganda. At the time of my birth, my parents were Salvation Army Officers, Pastors if you like, in charge of the work at the local 'Corps' (their Church) in one of England's famous pottery towns and had they known that their son was already practising an imaginary brass instrument as he lay in his pram, they would have been delighted.

Other memories of my childhood like having two slightly older sisters were not always so pleasant. I loved both Jennifer and Pauline dearly but at times it seemed that they would only use me as a patient in some fictitious hospital, themselves being either the doctor or the nurse. They would then cover me in bandages made from torn up old bed sheets and put red watercolour paint onto them to look like the blood was seeping through from imaginary wounds. It was a great relief when my younger brother David was born and I had someone else as well to spend my time with.

David was five years younger than myself and as we grew older I treasured the time spent with him helping him with his school homework or making model cars or castles for him from old cardboard boxes. The life of a Salvation Army Pastor or Officer was always a very busy one and dad was fully occupied in ministry so I became a sort of surrogate father to my younger brother especially during our school days. A powerful bond developed between us which remains to this day.

Family life was happy but very much centred around the varied Salvation Army activities at the Corps in Ilford, which was then a large town in the county of Essex and on the eastern edge of the capital city of London, England. This was before it was to be lost in the mass of suburbia known as Greater London.

I had a good childhood. There was a lot of love around and my parents' Christian testimony that they often shared with us and their lifestyle left a great impression on our young lives. Mum and dad would often relate the stories of their early Salvation Army ministry experiences in Wales where they were first appointed. Though engaged to be married they were forbidden by the SA authorities to get married until they had proved their 'separate calling' and so were appointed to different parts of South Wales.

Mum was only 19 when she was first commissioned as a young Captain. She was a member of the Torchbearer Session from the Denmark Hill Salvation Army Training College of London and was appointed to serve in the Rhondda Valley with an even younger girl, her Lieutenant, also fresh from the training college. Dad was elsewhere serving his probationary year but both were looking forward to getting married and being together soon.

These early years proved to be a baptism of fire for both of them, for it was the time of great hardship in Wales as the coal pits were closing one by one and there was no food on the villagers' tables. It was very much the same for my mother and father too. Yet God provided.

I remember one story in particular that my mother often retold us about the time when she and the little Lieutenant were living in the Welsh valleys during that awful time of the Great Depression of the 1930s. It's hard to imagine the sense of foreboding, of fear and hopelessness that my mother and her young assistant must have felt, away from home for the first time, having had a very short period of training and now plunged into a leadership role amongst tough miners, their wives and families looking to them for help in a time of real desperation.

The main industry of Wales was coal mining but as many were shutting down, the work that the villagers depended on simply disappeared overnight. There were such dire shortages and suffering. It went on for months and months. Unemployment in Wales reached a record level of 42.8%. Children had no shoes to wear and were dressed in old handouts. Often my mother would describe to us with tears in her eyes the abject poverty they all experienced. The Salvation Army just had to do something so these two young women, one seventeen and my mother nineteen, began to provide breakfasts for everybody every morning at the Salvation Army Hall.

The grateful villagers would crowd into the hall in families to eat their one meal of the day. This went on for months, the cost being covered from the small allowance that the SA Headquarters would send monthly to meet the personal needs of its serving officers. But it wasn't long before demand outgrew the supply and the money was simply not enough.

It was late at night and they had nothing to give the villagers the next morning for breakfast. But the training my mother had received, however brief, and the deep personal knowledge of God's love for them both provided the answer needed in that hour. They simply dropped to their knees in their two room terraced house and prayed for God's mercy and provision. What they said my mother never told me but the Father heard their cry and answered.

After some time of prayer there was a knock at the door of their little house. Nervously they went to see who was knocking at this late hour of the day. There was no one there but on the pavement in the dim street lamp light they saw a hamper, a huge straw hamper and it was full of food. It had a label tied to the wicker handle. It read, "For the two 'Angels of Mercy'".

It was stories and testimonies like these, forged in the crucible of suffering, demonstrating the provision of God and the triumph of their simple faith, that ignited a desire in my heart to know for myself 'His wonderful acts'.' *Lord increase my faith'* was my cry. It was only years later that I desired to know as much about His 'Ways' as I did His 'Acts', and even more so. Psalm 103:7 says "He made known His ways [of righteousness and justice] to Moses, but His acts to the children of Israel". Knowing Him and His ways was for Jesus the essence of eternal life for as He said in His prayer recorded in John 17 it was..."To know Him and He whom He has sent."

My father too would tell us about the many healing miracles he witnessed after praying for the sick or about the crippled man who walked again and whose crutches they hung on the wall of the Salvation Army Hall as a permanent reminder of God's goodness. These were always referred to as 'trophies of grace'.

However despite these powerful influences in my own life, by the time I was about seven years of age some unsettling emotional and spiritual characteristics were starting to emerge in my behaviour. I can remember feeling very insecure at times and very angry. I have vivid memories of moments when these feelings would overwhelm me. One, in particular, was very unpleasant and caused an outburst that upset the whole family.

Often as an eight year old, I would sit crossed-legged on the floor in the middle of our living room playing with my toy cars. I found this position most comfortable. A pleasant picture of doing just this is etched in my memory and I can recall it clearly.

We had all gathered together in the living room and I was sitting cross-legged in front of a small but oh so special 9-inch television set watching the coronation of Queen Elizabeth the Second. We were all there watching the pageantry and spender of this occasion, yet it was all happening miles away from where we all were. Amazing! Salvation Army salaries in 1952 were very small indeed so my parents must have scraped and saved so hard to buy this miracle box of new technology so we could all enjoy this nationally shared historic experience.

However, the other memory of sitting on that floor cross-legged is not so pleasant but it led to the point in my young life when I had to come face to face with the reality of my sin and of my need of a Saviour. I also needed healing from the hurts in my young heart too. I remember so well sitting on the floor there in the barely furnished living room. My ginger hair was still smartly parted and matched the colour of my freckles. I was wearing short grey trousers and was dressed in a short sleeved white shirt and a hand knitted sleeveless fair-isle jumper. But my freckled face was set ridged in absolute defiance and disobedience. Having been asked in a quite gentile way to go to bed, I would simply just refuse to budge.

Would I obey? No! Never! It was showdown time. I can even now sense how I felt then. I felt so very angry and rebellious but I didn't know why. I didn't want to be like this but I couldn't help it. I felt driven and out of control. Many a night this reoccurred until my poor mother was distraught beyond that which she could take.

One night this behaviour drove her to run out of the home sobbing hysterically leaving us all alone while she roamed the streets. Dad was still out at the 'Army' as we always referred to it. Mum did not return till early hours of the morning having just wandered around in tears. My dear father was so worried when he got home and found us all upset too waiting for mum to come back. Life did return to normal but something had to be done to stop this from ever happening again.

Of course I was always so very sorry afterwards. I remember how both my sisters and I would go to school that next day all with sore eyes from the tears of the night before. However, my parents had always taught us all to pray and they faithfully observed a 'family altar' each morning at breakfast time where at the table mum and dad would read a passage of the Bible and we would all pray the Lord's Prayer. But I, like my sisters, accepted that as normal and something we just did and it was of little significance.

Sometime later, after another similar traumatic episode my father called me to him and after asking me to sit down began to ask me some questions. It was getting near bedtime and I wanted to play in the garden but reluctantly I sat down. "Howard," he said. "You go to the Sunday school lessons don't you? What do you do there?" Silly question I thought. Why is he asking me? Surely he knows. He's an SA Officer. I gave some quick but flippant answers just to satisfy him, so I thought.

"Oh, we try to wind up our teacher, Miss Crab, by getting down on our hands and feet, tummies upwards, and we all begin to walk like a crab". I was lost for a moment in my thoughts picturing this act of ignorance and insensitivity and felt how unfortunate it was that she had been given such a bad surname.

My father's next question suddenly brought me back to reality and this 'interrogation'. "Well what do you learn about at Sunday School?" he asked. By now I had all that I could take but I loved my father enough not to want to dishonour him so I decided to show him that I had been listening at Sunday School. I could do this best by quoting the latest Bible verse Miss Crab had asked us to learn. It was John 3:16. "For God so loved the world that he gave his one and only Son, that whoever believes in Him shall not perish but have eternal life."

I thought that that would be it and I turned to proceed to go out to play in our garden. "Just a minute son," said dad. "That's great. Well done. The whole verse. Excellent, but tell me son, who is the world? If Jesus died on the cross to forgive the world, then who is the world?" A little impatiently I replied, "Well it's those in Africa, in India and here in England. It is for our neighbours and my friends and my aunts and my uncles. It's for my sisters. It's for you dad and for mum, and it's for me? For me? Did Jesus die for me? Then why am I such a naughty boy?"

It seemed confusing to me that if Jesus had died to take away my sin then why had I still got it? My Father's answer to my question was short but to the point. "Because you have never asked Him to do that, have you? To take it away," "Oh no dad. I haven't. Dad, how do I ask for that?" I cried. So led by my father, I knelt by the side of the dining room table and prayed a simple sinner's prayer one line at a time after him.

"Lord Jesus, I'm so sorry for all the things I've done wrong or thought, or felt, or said. Please forgive me. Thank you for dying on the cross for me. Please take my sin away now and come into my life as my Saviour and friend and change me. Amen" "Now, off to bed son, it's late," dad said and I went without any hesitation. It was so amazing.

That night I had a nosebleed and the pillowcase and sheets were stained with blood. When I awoke the next morning I was so upset because I realised that I had made my mother do so much washing.

I called my mum and with tears in my eyes I asked her to forgive me and then I realised, I WAS DIFFERENT! And, the anger had gone too.

I had been conceived naturally because of the love between my mother and father. I was born into an earthly family but

I was now born again because of the will and love of my Heavenly Father and because Jesus sacrificed His life for me. I had been placed into a new family too, my Heavenly Father's family.

My spiritual journey had begun. I had a new life. I could begin again. I didn't know then what sort of path it would be but I sensed I knew 'One' who did. There would be many exciting new experiences, truths and revelations along the way. I didn't know that the way would lead upwards, to answer the call to "come up higher," but right now though, I needed to train on the foothills.

Chapter 3: School Daze

"Before I formed you in the womb, I knew you, before you were born I set you apart; I appointed you." Jeremiah 1:5.

"For we are God's workmanship, created in Christ Jesus to do good works, which God prepared in advance for us to do." Ephesians 2:10.

You may be surprised by the title of this third chapter 'School Daze' and think that it should be 'Days' not 'Daze' but it's deliberate. This is because it best describes the sort of adolescent I was at this time. I was quite immature and still rather insecure, very much an attention seeker. As a result, in my first year at Mayfield Secondary Boys School, I became quite a show off. However, I also had a carefree personality and was very spontaneous which was a strange mix. Most of my early life was lived in a sort of superficial daze or even haze. I didn't process things in my mind very much and didn't 'engage' much with life in a conscious way. Life just went by.

That could and did lead to certain acts of irresponsibility and even stupidity but somehow I always bounced back. As I got older I began to feel that my life was very favoured and under a grace I didn't deserve. Whatever silly incident or irresponsible action I got involved with somehow always sorted themselves out. As a teenager my trust in God's love for me was very strong. Equally, my ability to take risks was too because of the lack of forethought or the love of excitement seemed to help my faith develop as I enjoyed believing in the seemingly impossible and in trusting God to the extreme.

This had certainly been influenced by my parents' example and testimonies. But now I was being strongly encouraged by the life and faith of my school's Religious Education teacher Mr. Dick Fry. He taught me RE and also ran the school Christian Fellowship Club which met after school once a week and to which all pupils were invited. I joined as soon as I could and thoroughly enjoyed the meetings. The films we watched there were so inspiring. The testimonies of people he invited to speak to us either in the lessons or at the Christian Fellowship were so challenging.

I remember on one occasion watching the Missionary Aviation Fellowship's film about the five missionaries who were murdered by the Auca Indians of Ecuador and watching the remarkable story of how these missionaries' wives went back to the same dried up river bed and found the Indians that had murdered their husbands and forgave them. These Auca Indians came to Christ as a result.

I also remember meeting Gladys Aylward the famous missionary to China who was made even more famous by the Hollywood film of her life 'The Inn of the Sixth Happiness' starring Ingrid Bergman. Listening to her testimony and watching the film about the MAF missionaries probably sowed the seed in my heart for the missionary call I was to receive later.

However, the showing of faith building films were not only reserved for the Christian Fellowship. Mr. Fry would also show these in his RE lessons. I so clearly remember sitting spell bound on a hard wooden school seat watching in the dark room a black and white Religious Film about the lives of people like William Carey, missionary to India, and of George Muller, the creator of the George Muller Children's homes in Bristol, UK. I'm not ashamed to say that I often shed a tear as I was 'strangely moved' at the wonder of Muller's faith and commitment to pray for everything he needed.

I'm so glad the room was blacked out because it hid my tears and my embarrassment from my peers. Muller would pray right through the night for whatever he needed. It made no difference whether it was for a breakfast for all the children for the following morning or for a single yarn of wool to fulfil a child's birthday present request.

The highlight of the Christian Fellowship's year was the Easter Mission that Mr. Fry would arrange in an Essex village and to which he would invite some of the senior Christian pupils so they could experience missionary life. Now because of my Salvation Army background I was quite used to giving a testimony at Sunday School or of marching through the street to read a scripture or give my testimony in a public place and oh, I so wanted to go on the Easter Mission but I was only 13 and still in the second year at Mayfield School. I begged Mr. Fry to let me go but despite my protest, he said I had to wait till I was much older. God had different plans. After just one more request by me, he finally relented and made an exception. I felt as if someone had given me a million pounds or dollars. I was going on a mission to preach the gospel, wow!

Some sixty and more years later, I can still look back and vividly picture myself standing in a circle in the centre of a village in Essex, singing hymns and giving testimonies to the passers-by and to those who stopped to listen. What a glorious experience it was and how wonderful it was to wake up that Easter Sunday morning on the hard chapel benches where we slept and could feel the sun beaming in through the daffodil adorned chapel windows. Resounding in my head would be the sound of "Jesus Christ is risen today, hallelujah!" What days! What memories! What a privilege!

I see now that all this was part of the preparation for the many missionary trips we would venture on in later seasons, to places as diverse as South Africa and the Philippines, South Korea and Cuba, Nepal, India and Pakistan, Italy and Germany or Liberia, Nigeria, Kenya, Malawi, Rwanda, Uganda, Burundi, Ghana or Togo, Cameroon or Egypt, and many, many more.

I'm glad to say that my 'daze' finally lifted and my secondary school education ended with a very satisfying set of O levels (Ordinary level) followed by three Advanced levels two years later, one in Religious Education, one in Engineering Drawing and one in Art practical and the History of Art.

When deciding what to study at 'A' level I wasn't sure whether God wanted me to follow a career as an Architect or Draftsman or enter the teaching profession as an Art and RE specialist or even train for the ministry so I chose these Advanced level courses to keep my options open. God however, already had a destiny for me which was written on my scroll in Heaven but my challenge was to discover it and follow what was written down on it. I wanted to fulfil all that was prepared for me beforehand.

Ephesians 2:10 "For we are God's workmanship, created in Christ Jesus to do good works, which God prepared in advance for us to do."

Psalm 139:16 "your eyes saw my unformed body. All the days ordained for me were written in your book before one of them came to be." This was not fate but destiny. I knew that my willingness to follow God's ways was what made the difference between fate and destiny. Fate was unavoidable but destiny was a choice. I had to opt into destiny.

I thank God that the Holy Spirit had already taught me that if I trusted in the Lord with all my heart and leaned not on my own understanding but in all ways acknowledge Him, then He would direct my paths. Proverbs 3:5-6.

I decided that God wanted me to go into the teaching career and after a successful time at university, I accepted my first teaching position at the very same Secondary school I had been a pupil at. The Headmaster had invited me to return and to teach RE and Art up to 'A' level in my old school. What an honour. So I actually stepped into Mr. Fry's teaching position, he was now retired and I began to lead the same Christian Fellowship once a week. Little did I know that a Holy Spirit Revival was going to descend down from heaven and half of the school would come to Christ.

But first let me record some of the lessons the Father wanted me to learn while I was in University.

Chapter 4: University and the Student life

"Do your best to present yourself to God as one approved, a workman who does not need to be ashamed." 2 Timothy 2:15

To some degree we children lived a fairly sheltered life at home with mum and dad. The rather strict but full Salvation Army life protected us from the 'less desirable influences' that we might have met at the nightclub or the snooker parlour. I was the first of our family to go to university and in that sense the first to taste the freedom and independence that was offered.

I had the chance of going to Durham University to study Theology but opted instead for Chester College which was part of Liverpool University and I took a Teacher Training Course. This was partly because it was near Wales, a part of the United Kingdom I had not previously visited and I would use Chester as a springboard to explore the beautiful Welsh countryside and especially the mountain ranges of Snowdonia.

My first college year I was in 'halls'. That meant I had a small room in one of the dormitory students' buildings on site. But I had my own key to my room and could come and go as I pleased, although the main door of the building was locked at 11pm. You could, however, always knock for someone to let you in who had a room on the ground floor. Visitors were not restricted and 'all night visitors' although not officially allowed were frequently seen leaving very early in the morning. Not that students went out their way to break the rules but it was knowing that there was little oversight of student activities that created that feeling of freedom.

In my second year I moved with fellow student Philip Clarke into a private let in the city outside the college precinct. This was less institutional and made you feel even more independent. Coming from my background this was a time of rapid growth and exciting new opportunities and challenges.

My first challenge in fact was to find a car and learn to drive.

Having just come from the Salvation Army Corps at Ilford in Essex to Chester and having played Bb Cornet in the Ilford Band, it seemed natural that I should begin to attend the local corps where I was now based. The Amy Officer and his wife felt a pastoral care for me and welcomed me into their home as often as I wanted to visit them.

Now, sitting on his runway was an Austin 7 Ruby 1936 model which he had bought but rarely used and so it was just parked there. It was a beauty. My grandmother in Buckingham near Oxford had one and would collect us in it from the station whenever Jennifer, Pauline and myself as kids were packed off to Grandma's for a holiday in the country. Oh the smell of the leather seats and the petrol fumes. The memory still lingers.

When Major Thomas heard of my need for a car he immediately offered me the Austin Ruby since he didn't need it anymore and what's more he didn't want anything for it. I was so grateful and so proud to own it. The car had large headlamps and cable brakes. Wow!

I learnt to drive on it. There was always some student with a licence that would sit beside me as I learnt. We had such fun. But it died and was actually impounded by the police at the Police Station in Coleford, Gloucestershire. This is because as I was driving down from Chester to my parents' home, then in London, with a fully licensed student friend by my side, the fumes began pouring out of the exhaust pipe and attracted the attention of a parked policeman. He promptly followed us and then flagged us down. He asked to see our driving licences. My friend showed his and I, ignorant as they come, remarked much to the shock of my friend, that I hadn't yet got one since I was only learning. I had no idea in my naivety that I too needed a licence albeit a provisional one.

The car was impounded and we were to make our way to London by some other means but return as soon as possible to Coleford Police Station complete with a provisional licence and then they would release the car. They let us off with a warning believing that this was a case of ignorance rather than deliberate unlawfulness but the fumes that the policeman had seen pouring out from the exhaust pipe of Ruby were a sign of something far much more sinister to come. Ruby died peacefully at a local scrapyard a month or so later.

If only I had known then what I know now, I'd have kept the car until I could have restored it even if it was years later.

Today that little treasure would be worth literally thousands and thousands!

In my third year at university I took a job during the summer break with my local council Road Works Dept. in Ilford. I was staying there during the holiday period with my parents. It was hot work tarmacing roads and laying pavements in the summer heat. I would return home at the end of the day, my work clothes filthy and smelling of bitumen, my face streaming with sweat and looking so black and dirty as if I had been in those Welsh coal mines my mother had spoken about.

Laying pavements was less strenuous and certainly far less dirty a job. If you are ever in Barking, London then visit Barking London Transport Underground Station and do have a look at the pavement outside the Station and you may well see the ones I laid though I doubt they are still the same ones I laid in 1964!

Cycling home one night from Barking to the neighbouring borough of Ilford and towards the end of that work experience, I happened to catch a glimpse of another amazing old car, a Riley Merlin 1937. It was parked beside a mechanic's garage. The next day I stopped to look at the sale sign and discovered that if I worked for just one more week I could afford the price. So very soon I was the proud owner of another beautiful old car painted in traditional British Racing Green and displaying huge round headlamps either side of the gleaming long bonnet. This bonnet had hinged lifting panels either side of it. A running board the length of the two doors left and right enabled you to step up and into the car and then sink into the leather seats. The window wipers were also hinged enabling the front windscreen to be wound up outward and almost horizontally.

I still hadn't passed my test yet but with a qualified driver beside me. I remember driving into college at Chester on my return feeling like the Lord of the manor. It was quite a talking point even in those days.

The horizontal windscreen proved to be so valuable as one day when driving back from a memorial service held in Stockport of a dear friend killed in a car crash, we hit a patch of dense fog or mist. We were worried because we were already late back and were concerned not to miss the lockout deadline.

Driving or rather fumbling in the fog at night with a car full of noisy fellow students was not a pleasant or a helpful experience. It was difficult to see. But then with our green and white college scarves wrapped around our faces and flapping in the wind over our shoulders and the windscreen wound up into full horizontal position with headlights blazing we were able to drive at some speed and eventually got back just in time. We arrived safely in this beloved Riley Merlin but in our imaginations it was as if we had raced on desert camels. The comparison is clear. With our scarves flapping behind us we galloped with speed through the dark night as if we were Lawrence of Arabia himself.

These were great memories but college life and its new freedoms also presented very real temptations. God however was always there walking through them with me. As He says in Psalm 23:4 "Though I walk through the valley of the shadow of death, I will fear no evil." Our Father uses all challenges as means of testing us and maturing us. As we've said already 'there is no testimony without a test.'

On one occasion a real temptation was presented to me in the way of a relationship with a young lady.

At a Student's Ball I attended at Alsager College for Girls in Derbyshire I had seen a girl who had recently won her College's Beauty Queen competition and then I heard that she was planning on coming to the Student's Ball at our college in the next few weeks. Wow! There was a buzz around the student halls. Every male student fancies his chances to gain a date with her and I could just not resist this challenge. My ego would not allow me to. I had no peace, so despite the fact that I was a Christian and a regular member of the College Christian Union, I decided I would enter the competition.

I attended the Ball that next week AND danced with her AND she accepted my request to date. But this so-called victory was 'allowed' for the purposes of God and was NOT because of my good looks, attractiveness or courting expertise. God wanted to teach me a valuable lesson. We began to phone each other whenever I could get a space on the one students' public phone-line. We didn't have mobile phones in those days.

She agreed to come over to Chester to see me and I anticipated the visit with very mixed feelings. I knew I was in rebellion.

That date did actually go quite well but somehow my heart was not in it. I knew I was being disobedient. She didn't know the Lord at all and we had simply nothing in common. When she had left to return home I felt bad. I got down on my knees in my student's room and wept before the Lord in repentance. I would end the relationship and I promised the Lord that I would never ever date a nonbeliever but would allow Him to look after the 'relationship department'. 2 Corinthians 6:14 "Be not unequally yoked together with unbelievers: for what fellowship has righteousness with unrighteousness and what communion has light with darkness?"

During University, God demonstrated His favour towards me in so many ways. As part of our training, we had to do a period of teaching practice. Not far from Chester and in the middle of the Irish Sea, was a small island that belonged to the UK called the Isle of Man and it was there and Douglas Grammar School in particular that I was appointed for my second year teaching practice. It was one of the best teaching practice postings.

The famous TT motorbike races were held there every year and we were there for the whole month before that event. The race is run on the narrow roads and lanes all around the island. The teaching practice was great and I thoroughly enjoyed it. The pupils were lovely and the island's scenery was amazing but the day we were planning to leave, the weather changed from glorious sunshine to heavy rain and occasional mist. The TT race is only postponed or cancelled under severe weather conditions but on the other hand the small ferry boat to the mainland is not allowed to sail unless the sea is reasonably calm and visibility good.

So to our delight we were told after our practice had ended to remain at the hotel until the weather improved and then return to university. The school holiday had now begun, we could not extend our teaching practice so we enjoyed a free holiday at the college expense. And, because the TT race was beginning that coming week and the hotel where we stayed was on the race circuit, we had front row seats for an iconic European motorbike race. The Lord's favour indeed.

This was not the last time I was to enjoy the delights of the Isle of Man. I was to return very soon on a mission assignment from the Lord. He had something more to teach me about obedience and of His ability to provide resources supernaturally when needed. But first I needed to be shown my selfishness.

I was sitting in the students' refectory towards the end of our third term, having just had breakfast. Although I lodged out of college in Chester city, like many other students, we were allowed to have all meals at the refectory. The food was great and the breakfasts in particular, outstanding. I can still smell the bacon, the sausages, the baked beans marinated in tomato sauce and see clearly the fried or poached eggs, their huge golden yokes set like blazing suns against the pure white surrounds. Mmmmmm!

Our conversation was centred around what we were all planning to do during the long holiday that was fast approaching. I was so impressed by the dedication and heart for the mission that my Christian student friends demonstrated as they shared about their plans. A month with YWAM in India, a period of service at an orphanage in Kenya, a time working with the London City Mission in Inner London.

I felt so convicted. I realised that I was so selfish. I was so ashamed. I went home to my own room, shut the door behind, and knelt down beside my bed, and wept. There and then I recommitted my life to Jesus and promised that if the Lord would lead me I would go anywhere and do anything He wanted me to do that coming summer vacation.

So began a time of seeking the Lord and of searching through Christian magazines to pray over advertisements which requested candidates who could accept short term appointments for mission or to serve at Christian holiday homes or hotels.

It was not long before one advert stood out as if it were written in neon lights. It was for a young Christian man or woman who played guitar and could lead worship and give short Bible messages, to serve as a member of staff at a Christian hotel in, yes, Douglas on the Isle of Man. It was for late July and August into September. I felt so much at peace about this that I applied and was accepted. So a few weeks later I was back in beloved Douglas feeling so strongly the anointing of God in my life.

I suppose the best way to describe the job was to compare it to that of a 'Red Jacket' member of staff at a large commercial holiday hotel complex whose sole purpose is to make sure that all holiday makers have a great time. The difference was that I was to bless them spiritually too, help them to grow in Christ and if they didn't know the Lord personally, then lead them to Him.

It was such a marvellous time in my life and I saw so many come to Christ during those months or receive prayer for healing. I certainly learnt that joy comes from being obedient and that in laying down one's life for Jesus you actually gain LIFE, His life in you. Colossians 1:27 "To them God has chosen to make known among the Gentiles the glorious riches of this mystery, which is Christ in you, the hope of glory."

But there was one more deeply profound experience that God had for me before I returned home from the Isle of Man. During this time in Douglas, He was determined to affirm all those testimonies that my mum and dad had shared with us about God's provision for our physical and financial needs as well as for our spiritual needs.

My time there was quickly coming to an end and although we didn't receive a wage we did get a little pocket money to meet any personal needs. Everything else was catered for. But I did need my ferry and train fare home in a week and I had saved enough to buy those tickets.

My father had sent a letter which was a request for a certain amount of money to cover the cost of stationery that I had used during the previous term. I didn't have to send it immediately and I needed all I had to buy my tickets home first. But the Spirit of God impressed upon me that I should send it and gave me the verse Matthew 6:33 "But seek first His Kingdom and His righteousness and all these things will be given to you as well." So I bought a postal order from the local Post Office and sent it off to university not knowing how I could afford my fares home.

Now one of my first responsibilities every morning at the hotel was to ring a small bell at the breakfast table and pray or say grace. One day several people were a little late so I waited a while for them and as I began reaching for the bell, I saw an envelope placed against it addressed to me with the postmark, Northern Ireland. I tentatively picked up the envelope and opened it. There inside was just a folded blank piece of paper wrapped around several English pound notes adding up to exactly the amount of money I had sent away the day before. I was so shocked that I had to sit down and ask someone else to say grace. Truly God had provided.

These things ignited a longing within me to know more about the power of God. It created hunger but also dissatisfaction with my own Christian experience. Surely there was more than what I had already? More to receive. More to experience.

It was quite remarkable, however, that I was unwilling to confess publicly any weakness of character or lack of anything in my Christian life. I was a proud young man still and very much a self-made person. I knew little about the 'death of self' or of being 'crucified with Christ'. Pride and the desire for a good public image were the biggest stumbling blocks in my life. But God was working hard on that department and was about to deal with this in no uncertain manner.

I knew I had pride in my heart. The Lord reminded me of when the famous American evangelist, Billy Graham, was visiting England and was holding a Crusade near my home at the Ford Car Manufacturing Works in Romford Essex. I decided to go. I was only twelve years of age and loved the Lord Jesus and was keen that my school friend Neville would accept Jesus as his Saviour so I invited him to come with me. We travelled on the London red double-decker bus service that operated as far out in Essex as Romford and we went and heard Billy Graham preach.

It was an amazing sight to see tens of thousands of people gather in the marquee or stand for miles outside in the open air just to hear a preacher. But his preaching was captivating and both Neville and I were deeply moved even though we were still so young.

When the famous Billy Graham 'appeal' was given, we had to respond. Through the loud speakers we heard, "Get up from your seats and come forward saying, "Just as I am without one plea but that His blood was shed for me and that thou bidst me come to thee, Oh Lamb of God, I Come". Thousands of people flocked forward to receive Jesus and to be counselled. They were led to accept God's forgiveness through Christ and asked Him into their lives, just as I had done with my father four years previously. And amongst the thousands responding were two school boys called Howard and Neville.

However, as far as I was concerned I was only there with Neville helping him make his decision and I made sure that the counsellor knew this. The strange thing was that this lady counsellor would not accept my protestations. She insisted on talking to me first saying that God had told her that He wanted me to submit entirely to Him. But my pride would still not allow me to 'bend the knee'. God is so persistent and that pride was finally laid at the foot of the cross some years later, way after university days at a Salvation Army meeting in Walthamstow, London.

The Salvation Army in the mid-1960s had ventured into pop music to be more relevant to young people of the day and they had created a pop group called The Joy Strings. In fact, they were very good and appeared on the famous British television pop show called Top of the Pops. They were so popular that they scored number one on the charts. The Joy Strings were having a gospel concert in Walthamstow around 1967 and I went along with my brother David.

I was now 23 and had recently started teaching. It was a time in England when we had two very distinct rival youth gangs, the Mods and the Rockers, who would often meet on a beach somewhere to fight each other, such as Brighton Beach one hundred miles south of London. They would drive there in gangs, the Mods on Lambretta scooters and the Rockers on Motorbikes. When I arrived at the Walthamstow Salvation Army hall for the Pop Concert I went upstairs to sit on the balcony and I found that it was packed with Mods and Rockers jeering at each other.

Amazingly when the concert started everyone quieted down as the presence of God filled the place. At the end of the concert, people were once again invited to leave their seats and walk to the front and stand or kneel in front of the stage as a sign that they wanted to receive Jesus as their Saviour. I was thrilled and amazed as several Mods and then Rockers would come to the front and kneel side by side in submission to the Lord Jesus.

And then it happened.

"Howard. You go down there to the front." I knew it was God speaking to me.

"But I am saved and I do love you already," I replied.

"If you love Me, then obey Me," He said.

"But I'm here in my Salvation Army uniform. And in front of my brother who thinks the world of me. What will he think? What will everybody think? that I'm a sinner?"

There it was. Out in the open. Clear, unadulterated blatant pride.

Once more I felt exposed, ashamed and so unworthy. "Ok, Lord. I'll do this for you. But only this week I read an article about people who keep going forward for salvation at meetings time and time again and it makes a mockery of it. Are you really telling me to do this in front of all these people and from this balcony all the way down to the front of the stage? Please be merciful to me and if you are asking this of me then get that man in front of me there to turn around and tell me to go out. Then I'll know it's You".

That moment one of The Joy Strings spoke through the microphone saying that they realised everything had gone on much longer than expected so suggested that if anyone needed to leave to go home, to feel free to do so. At that very moment, the man in front of me got up and looked at me and I freaked. He turned and started to make his way toward the stairs to go home, but he forgot his hat and as he was coming back for it he reached over towards me and looked deep into my eyes and said," Hey son. You should be out in front, shouldn't you? Good night." And he was gone.

I immediately told my brother that I was going down to the front so I wouldn't back down and stood up and made my way out down the stairs and towards the stage. When I got there I knelt down waiting for someone to come and to speak with me as they did for others but no one came. I realised that this was only between God and myself. In the quietness, I surrendered. After a while, I got up and returned to my seat but that old stubborn spirit of pride had gone and I could sense that something good had taken place deep within my heart.

Jesus is looking for a willing and submissive bride. She must learn to honour and obey Him in everything. My journey towards the Bridegroom had moved a little further forward but there was still yet much more distance to be travelled.

Chapter 5: Lord, There Must be More?

"Did you receive the Holy Spirit when you believed?" he asked them. They answered, "No, we have not even heard that there is a Holy Spirit." Acts 19:2.

"And these signs will accompany those who believe: In My name, they will drive out demons: they will speak in new tongues; they will pick up snakes with their hands; and when they drink deadly poison, it will not hurt them at all; they will place their hands on sick people and they will get well." Mark 16: 17-18.

Despite the fact that God was clearly moving in my life and dealing with me, I was also aware that there was still something missing in my Christian experience. The times of knowing God's miraculous power and presence were still too infrequent. I longed for a deeper walk with God and the knowledge of the presence of the Holy Spirit upon and within me. I had often questioned things like 'speaking in tongues and the baptism in the Holy Spirit. But this subject was something that was not discussed openly within the Salvation Army circles in those days. I'm so glad to say that is not the case now and today there is a real hunger for things of the Spirit within 'Army' circles.

For me, the quest for Baptism in the Spirit began with a fascination with tongues and with the supernatural gifts of the Spirit in general. Then it developed into a study of Acts of the Apostles to see how the early Church moved in that

Spirit. Finally, 1 was convinced that these things were still for us today and I wanted and needed to be a part of the 'Renewal or Charismatic Movement' that was touching most parts of the global Church at that time.

I saw that the Baptism of the Spirit was in Scripture. It was the experience of the early Church and Jesus had promised He would send the Holy Spirit to come in His place who would bring these 'spiritual gifts' with Him and this seemed also to be what God was doing within His Church at that time.

But God had gone ahead in preparing the way for me, as He always does for every one of His children. While I was still at university He arranged for me to share digs with a tongues-speaking Pentecostal called Phil Clarke who hailed from Stockport, England. I was intrigued to hear Phil speaking in tongues quietly beside his bed during his personal prayer time.

Then one evening at the College Christian Union we met the Reverend Norman Meeten, an Anglican priest from Everton who shared his testimony of being baptised in the Holy Spirit while talking with two elderly woman parishioners. Norman's testimony left such an impression on my life. He came dressed in a black rolled necked jumper over his priestly 'dog collar' and with blazing eyes shared his experience of being drenched in what he described as 'cool clear water' being poured out over his head and down over his body one day as he was simply speaking to two elderly lady members of his congregation.

He explained how he had reached a point in his life where he had to know more of the reality of God or he was going to quit the Ministry. This experience changed everything for him. His preaching changed. It had power and interest. He felt so confident and excited and when he prayed for any sick church member they got healed.

God was now bringing a convergence of certain experiences about the Holy Spirit to my life that would result in myself being baptised in the Spirit. The first was befriending Pentecostal student Philip Clarke, the second hearing Rev. Norman Meeten and the third and final experience of being so wonderfully 'cornered' by the Holy Spirit at a meeting at the Elim Pentecostal Church in Ilford.

I love the way the Holy Spirit traps us sometimes and finally gets His way. It may feel painful for us at the time but it's His love for us that causes Him to do what He does. So how was it that I got gloriously trapped or cornered into submission and finally received my Baptism in the Spirit? One of the difficulties I was having was that I had asked God if He would fill me with the Spirit whilst I was on my own and not when in public. Consequently, I was resisting the leadings of God in my life because I was laying down my conditions. It had to be without anyone 'laying hands' on me I had said.

A local Baptist Church Minister, Pastor Henry Tyler, had recently received the gift of tongues and was sharing his testimony at the local Pentecostal after-church meeting that Sunday night. My Christian colleague at Mayfield School who attended the Elim Church had told me about the meeting and invited me along. My dear Tricia, at that time my fiancé, was visiting me at my parents' home for the weekend and so we went along together. Tricia and I had discussed Baptism several times.

It was a good talk by Rev. Tyler and afterwards people were invited to ask questions. I raised my hand and asked whether in order to receive the Baptism of the Holy Spirit, you had to have someone lay their hands on your head and pray for you. Rev. Tyler answered simply "No. You can be on your own but if the Lord says that it is to be by the laying on of hands then that's the way it must be". That was just the answer I didn't want to hear. I sensed the Lord was closing in on the catch. All my resistance was being worn away.

After the meeting Tricia and I made our way to the door to go home. As we shook the hand of the steward he asked us who we were and where we were from. My reply set the trap that God had prepared for us. "We are from the Salvation Army up the road but we are seeking the Baptism of the Holy Spirit," I said. "You don't need to wait," the steward replied. "Come along with me and we will lay our hands on you and pray for you." And he grabbed my arm with Tricia following and pulled me with him toward a small office where several others gathered around us and prayed, each laying their hands upon our heads.

Tricia immediately burst into tongues and I soon followed. Wow, we were now really baptised in the Spirit and we made our way home trying to get our heads around what had just happened. Soon after that I was baptised in water as well in simple obedience to the Lord's command because I wanted to be able to fulfil all He wanted of me as a teacher at Mayfield School. I returned to school the next day to join my Christian colleague Brian Davies full of expectation as to what the Lord was going to do.

You may wonder how I had met dear Tricia and how she came to know the Lord.

You will remember that at the end of my time at university I had dated a non-Christian girl from another College. So meeting a girl called Tricia at the twenty-first birthday party of a mutual friend and sensing an attraction towards her I became very concerned. Tricia was a petite, very tanned, pretty young woman who was studying music at the Royal College of Music, London where Denise, whose birthday it was, also studied. The party was in a local church hall and when Denise asked both Tricia and myself to come back to her home to see her presents after the party I had to face the fact that something was pulling in my heart strings and I cried out to the Lord for help.

"Lord, You know that I've promised you that I would never again date a non-Christian and I sense that Tricia doesn't know you as her Saviour so what do I do?" I heard His Voice saying, " It's OK Howard but put me first, Ruthlessly, and go slowly. So whenever we wanted to see each other on any weekend from then on, Tricia would have to come to Ilford and attend the Salvation Army meetings since I was still attending there regularly and playing the cornet in the Salvation Army band.

It was clear Tricia was not yet a Christian but we talked long about Jesus and faith and often discussed the sermons together after a Sunday service. I never ever challenged her as to what she believed but just treated her as already a believer because I knew that since God had chosen her and told me that it was OK to date her but "acknowledge Him in all our ways" then He "would make all things work together for good" because He always "does all things well".

Her own salvation came unexpectedly one evening when we were going to bed at my parent's house. I asked if she might like to join in my prayer time in my room before she retired. We knelt down beside the bed and I shared a short passage of scripture I had felt led to read together. It was Romans 12:1 -19.

I had intended to read all the verses but I had only read the first few verses when Tricia burst into tears and said to me, "I'm not a Christian. I've never presented myself as a living sacrifice to Him as it says there."

Oh the conviction of the Holy Spirit. It's so convincing and transforming if the right response is made. For Tricia the perfect response was made. I knew Tricia enough by now to know she was a very independent person and needed to make her own decisions. So I explained how to accept Jesus and present yourself to Him as that living sacrifice through confession of sin and repentance. I suggested that she went to her own room and did what we discussed on her own. In the morning she was as the Bible says, "a new creature in Christ Jesus" and now some months later she too was also baptised in the Holy Spirit.

We felt released into a new anointing and felt His power and authority in our lives. This authority was to be tested very quickly for me at the house that I was renting in Rutland Road, nearer the centre of Ilford. I had moved out of my parents' home in order to flow with what God was doing because school evangelism and local church work seemed to merge into one and my house tended to be open to all and ministry continued day and night. It was not without spiritual opposition and enemy resistance but His power and authority dealt with all attempts of the enemy to derail the purposes of God. This showed itself so clearly soon after moving into my own rented flat in Ilford.

A fellow student from Chester College who had a teaching post in a nearby Greater London School and who was supposed to be a Christian, had moved into the house with me to help share the rent. But it soon became clear that this was a ploy of Satan to interfere in what God wanted to achieve. My friend would drink and I sensed he was taking drugs. Guys from the streets or local gangs would just drop in and it was obvious that they were seeking for something or 'someone,' His name was Jesus.

My friend would always appear at a very spiritually significant moment in a conversation that I was having with a group of youths and interrupt it. One night he entered the kitchen where I was talking with three boys and made flippant remarks. I was angry in my spirit and turned to look at him and commanded him to stop and be bound in Jesus name. He left the kitchen immediately and went to lie on his bed in the bedroom but as he lay down found himself literally bound. He simply couldn't move. I only discovered this when after the boys had left I found my fellow lodger still on his bed begging me to set him free. This dramatic demonstration of the real spiritual battles that were going on behind the scene was not only evident at home but we witnessed it at school too.

As the sense of the presence of God increased in the school, the opposition increased too, although there was never a sense of fear or foreboding, rather a sense of excitement and exhilaration. Prayer meetings increased accordingly. We held one for the pupils every day at lunch hour and since we had two dinner sittings for lunch we had two prayer meetings each day, in shifts.

Mayfield was a government Secondary Boys' School and most of the boys came from non-Christian homes and didn't belong to a local church. In fact, most had never been to church. Our School Christian meetings *were their church.* Soon all the boys were baptized in the Spirit and spoke in tongues and the prayer meetings just took off. There was such power present. The boys between 11 and 16 would ask whether they could use tongues in the meeting especially if they didn't know what to say but knew the subject that they wanted to pray about. The answer of course was, Yes. They also asked whether they had to wait for each other or if they could all pray at the same time and aloud and whether they had to sit still or could they walk around and pray?

So we decided to discuss before we prayed what we felt the Lord wanted us to talk to Him about and make a list on the blackboard and then all pray about those things together. We would do so from that list one at a time until the person in charge indicated that it was time to move on to the next subject for prayer. This way we would have some order in the meeting but freedom too.

So what we experienced was vibrant, active, rather noisy but oh such powerful prayer. Some boys would be standing against the classroom wall praying fervently rocking backward and forwards like the Jews at the Wailing Wall in Jerusalem. Others would be walking around praying out loud in English or in tongues.

If you have ever been to Africa and been with African people praying then you would have recognized the same things happening in their meetings. So later when I first went on a mission to Uganda and joined the believers in prayer it seemed as if I had been there before, but it had been in my classroom in Mayfield School years and years previously.

Prayer is always so central to the work of God. It was for us. My colleague Brian and I would meet every morning before school at 8 am to intercede for the boys and to call upon God to send revival- and revival He sent.

During that season we saw hundreds come to Christ. In fact, at one time half the school had received Jesus as their Saviour, and people were healed spontaneously in the lunchtime prayer meetings and at the weekly after-school Christian Fellowship meetings. For example, I caught one boy in the prayer meeting one day heavily banging his plastered arm which was supposed to be broken on the school desk shouting, "Look, Sir. God has just healed my arm." But healing would happen in the corridors too.

I was on my way to the school dining room buildings one lunchtime where I was on duty and as I walked down the corridor I saw a boy called Colin who had only the previous week accepted Christ. Colin was coming towards me. He was about thirteen. What I didn't know was that Colin suffered from epilepsy fits and was on Phenobarbital. As he approached us, he plunged into a fit and we ran and grabbed him before he hit the floor. He was still conscious but shaking violently so we carried him into the nearest classroom while I was repeating to him, "Colin. Colin. Call on the name of Jesus. You got saved last week. You are His now. Call Jesus! Jesus! Jesus!"

When we got into an empty classroom we sat Colin at the teacher's desk, laid our hands upon him, and prayed in Jesus name for healing and as if hit by a thunderbolt, Colin's fit immediately ceased and he shot up into the air. He was, in that instant, completely healed and returned to normal. He was so well that I sent him off and out into the playground until his dinner shift was called. A few minutes later I passed him in the playground rushing around like a lunatic, enjoying a game of chase with the others.

"What are you doing Colin?" I cried. "You have just been unwell. Come here!"

But I immediately saw my stupidity, my fear and unbelief rising up and denying the finished work of Christ. This finished work was completed 2000 years ago on the cross and I was so ashamed. "Oh, I'm so sorry Colin. Of course, God has healed you and that means completely. So, go on son, and prove it. Go and run as fast as you can around the playground.", and he did. But there is a rider to that story because God wanted the boys at the second shift prayer meeting to have reason to increase their faith.

I went into the dining room and began my duty of overseeing the pupils' meals. Colin was now sitting at one of the tables tucking into a plate full of food. Suddenly he clasped his head in his hands and was in obvious pain. The Spirit of God immediately said "Counterfeit. Demonic Counterfeit". So, I sent Colin with a friend to help him, back up to the prayer meeting to get the boys to pray for him whilst I got someone to cover my dinner duty. Then I would join them.

When I arrived in the prayer room the boys were all gathered around Colin and praying fervently for him. Suddenly he shot up into the air once again within the circle of boys shouting "Hallelujah! Hallelujah! I'm healed!" From that day onwards Colin never had another fit and all the boy's faith had 'shot up' in strength too, even higher than Colin had that day.

We also witnessed miracles of deliverance from demons which I refuse to share in detail here because they were literally not of this world. Such ministry did not take place within school but were the result of knowing the pupils through the school Christian Fellowship and as such were linked to school. These experiences were more reminiscent of a Hollywood horror movie than of what took place in a normal London Suburb. Also I want this book and the stories in it to be accessible and acceptable to all including those of more traditional theology and particularly for those with little or no faith at all.

To ask even an experienced Christian to believe such stories might present a real challenge but could be a step too far for others and I don't want to place any obstacles in people's way. Also others might legitimately accuse me of abusing my position as a teacher in a government school where such activities originated from. I could also be accused of exerting too much unhelpful and overtly religious pressure upon vulnerable children.

Be that as it may, certainly the culture in the UK was much more Christian in those days and Religious Education in schools was predominantly biblically based. But miracles of healing, conversations with demons and their resistance to leave the person in whom they lived and the strong presence of God felt in the school, were real enough to us. It was our everyday experience and the transformation in the lives of those saved, delivered or healed bears testimony to the value of what was happening.

A Journey of Ascent Towards the Bridegroom

Chapter 6: A Marriage Made in Heaven

"There is a time for everything and a season for every activity under heaven" Ecclesiastes 3:1.

It was Saturday, August 5th, 1967. The quaint church of St Giles, Ickenham glistened in the bright summer sunshine. The freshly cut grass that surrounded the church and framed the ancient gravestones gave a picture-postcard backdrop for our wedding that day. My parents, wearing their full Salvation Army Uniform, took part in the marriage service and we made our vows to one another in front of a church filled with friends and relatives. It was a wonderful day full of God's blessing and overshadowed by His presence. It marked the end of one season in our lives and the beginning of another.

Months before, I had known that my time at Mayfield Secondary School was coming to an end and God was calling us into marriage and eventually to a new life as a family on the other side of London. This would mean me moving schools from Essex on the east side of London to Middlesex on the west where Tricia had her first teaching post. She had been appointed to a tough school near London Airport and was finding it extremely difficult. I decided to join her at her school as soon as possible to support her. I was soon appointed as an RE teacher at Townmead Comprehensive School in Middlesex.

64

I knew how important marriage was to God but I didn't know then, as I know now, that the central theme of all biblical scripture was marriage and the marriage relationship, firstly between a man and a woman as in Genesis, then between God and Israel, and ultimately between Christ and His Church.

God would be watching how I treated my bride as I joined myself to her for indeed it was a picture of the relationship between Christ and His Bride.

Years later when I was on a mission in Africa I was ministering about the Bride of Christ and was made aware that some of the African Pastors who were present at the conference were not treating their wives very well. In fact some of these lovely women were being abused in all sorts of ways. And as far as the members of the Pastor's congregation were concerned who were part of Jesus' own Bride, they were not caring for them in the way Jesus would like.

The Pastors were listening to the Bridal message and nodding in agreement but still not caring for the needs of the people God had given to them to serve. Suddenly I heard Jesus say in my spirit, "Tell them. Do not touch My Bride unless you are in a right relationship with yours". Their marriage relationship with their own bride had to be a reflection of Jesus' intense love and care for His. Each member of their congregation was part of His Bride and they ultimately were only caring for her, assisting in developing her faith and love for Him so they could be mature. Their aim should be like Apostle Paul's, 'to present her as a pure virgin (bride) to Christ' 2 Corinthians 11:2.

A few years after arriving in Hillingdon I joined the staff of Barnhill School in Hayes Middlesex, a neighbouring borough, and again started a students' Christian Union or Fellowship for the pupils. But the time I had at Mayfield Secondary School will always be very special to me because it was not only my own first teaching appointment but was also as you will remember where I had been a pupil myself. But more importantly it was where we had experienced so much of God's anointing and power and presence amongst us whether in the classroom lessons or at the pupils' Christian Fellowship meetings.

It wasn't too long after I left, that the school changed its status and form, as part of the Government's reorganisation programme of Secondary Education, and with it Mayfield School as I knew it closed. We had sensed very strongly the Lord's guidance in making this move to Hillingdon and His provision and His protection went before us. The Lord provided a lovely semi-detached house for us on a 100% mortgage agreement with the local council.

We had two rooms and a kitchen downstairs and three bedrooms and a bathroom upstairs. The house had a small backyard and a large triangular garden at the side which was surrounded by a tall privet hedge. I would keep this hedge clipped tight and trim by using an electric hedge cutter every so often and it was during a regular cut that we saw evidence of God's wonderful protection on our lives. God's protection came this time in the form of an angelic visitation.

I had placed my tall step ladder where I wanted to start cutting and made sure the long electric lead to the plug inside the house was safely placed. Unfortunately, as I was cutting the hedge I turned and caught the lead in the blades. There was a huge blue flash and I was thrown off the ladder and crashed onto the pavement. My injuries were slight but I was rather shaken.

I went indoors to mend the lead in the two places where it had been cut by joining the electric wires back together and sat down on the floor in the hallway and began to strip the wires of their outer rubber casing. Very stupidly I used my teeth to do this because I had no scissors or wire strippers with me. The house was still empty as it was being prepared for our marriage.

The repair seemed to be going well and I had joined one already. I had also joined two of the three wires of the remaining cut and was about to join the last wire. I had only one wire to join now. It was then that I pricked my finger on the end of the last wire, so I thought. "Ooooh, that's sharp!" I cried out. But it was then that I realised I had not pricked my finger at all but had actually received a slight electric shock. Immediately I traced the wires that I had previously had in my mouth several times, back to the plug and the electric socket in the kitchen and I was aghast.

"Oh no, it's still plugged in and switched on. It's LIVE!" I cried out. "Oh Lord, I'm so sorry and so stupid". I should have been seriously hurt and possibly received burns and even damaged the organs in my body. But it was then that I sensed the awesome presence of a huge angelic being, twelve to fifteen feet tall so it seemed, standing and peering down at me from above and over my shoulder. "Silly little man. Be more careful!" I heard him say.

I knew I had had an angelic visitation. My heart was so full of gratitude to God for appointing one of these awesome created beings to watch over me. The Bible affirms that this is God's provision for us all. Psalm 91:11 "For he will command his angels concerning you to guard you in all your ways."

The second experience of God's protection was in appreciating more of His authority in casting away a demonic presence that was so strong in our new home and was hovering halfway up the staircase. We sensed it and smelt it as soon as we moved in. It was weird but so real, a putrid smell that came at any time it chose to and took us by surprise.

We rationalised the experience and eliminated all possible natural causes even getting the Gas Technicians to come and test for a gas leak. Finally we decided it was a spiritual matter and that some demon from hell was trying to disturb our peace. We didn't know well the people who had previously lived in our new house or what they had been involved in. Many activities can be the means of inviting demonic spirits in or to invade our human territory and disturb, oppress and even possess a person or a place.

So, we decided we would strengthen our faith, recognise the authority that God had given us as believers over such demons and trust the Lord to guide us. We planned that both

Tricia and myself would pray together against this the next time the smell presented itself and so see it go.

But the next night around 7pm when I was out at a youth meeting the putrid smell returned. Tricia was on her own but she decided to get her Bible and clutching it nervously approached the stairs and commanded the 'thing' to go, 'in Jesus' name', and immediately the smell disappeared and the demon left much to Tricia's encouragement and delight.

This was such a boost to our faith and the spiritual world became so much more a reality. Ephesians 6:12 "For our struggle is not against flesh and blood, but against the rulers, against the authorities, against the powers of this dark world and against the spiritual forces of evil in the heavenly realms." James 4:7 says, "Resist the devil, and he will flee from you." After that deliverance or exorcism the house felt altogether different. We soon made the place our home.

However we hadn't yet decided on our 'spiritual' home or church. A local place for regular worship was as much a priority for us as was the cleansing from demons of our physical home. So some time earlier while I was preparing the house for our married life I asked the Lord what local church He wanted us to serve and to worship at. I decided to visit the churches in the area on a Sunday and see how the Lord led.

Although I had left the Salvation Army years before and was no longer a Salvationist, I still appreciated the joy of the Army and the music of the Brass Bands and the choirs that they call 'Songsters'. So, not wanting to close that option down I felt I ought at least to go along to the local Salvation

Army Corps at Hillingdon which was nearest to where we lived and 'try it out' so to speak.

It was there one Sunday morning that I met a young captain called Captain John Larson. He was the officer in charge at the Hillingdon Corps and I was to become in time a close friend of his. The Sunday I visited John preached about the Holy Spirit and how we needed to be filled full of His power and presence. I was so blessed.

My father had become well known in Salvation Army circles as the SA Historian and had worked at the Editorial Department and on the Doctrine Council. He was based at the headquarters of the Salvation Army in Queen Victoria Street, London, near St Paul's Cathedral.

He also taught SA history at the Training College and took trainee Officers called Cadets on tours around London that William Booth, the Founder, had known. John would have met my father on these tours and attended his lectures.

But although this provided a link between us it was John's passion for more of the Spirit that impressed me and which was so clearly evident from his message that morning. After introducing myself to John and saying how blessed I was by his sermon I shared that I too had a longing for more of the Holy Spirit. So we agreed to meet regularly one morning a week in my unfurnished house to pray and wait upon the Lord for an outpouring of His Spirit.

We had such wonderful times together in the presence of the Lord and this began a friendship that has lasted all these years since. Captain John Larson went on to become the

British Commissioner of the Salvation Army in charge of all the work in the UK and then eventually the General Superintendent in charge of all the Salvation Army work throughout the world. It has been an honour to know him and pray for him over the years.

Although I kept my link with Hillingdon Corps, the Lord eventually led Tricia and myself to worship at St. Giles Anglican Church down the road in Ickenham where we had been married. We joined the community of St. Giles and started a CYFA Youth Group (Church Youth Fellowship Association) as a mid- week Youth meeting.

These were amazing times. Many students came along to join CYFA from the secondary school where I was teaching in Hayes; those who had come to know the Lord as their Saviour through either the RE Lessons or the Christian Union meetings. Oh it was such a glorious time at CYFA experiencing the presence of God together. We didn't play games or offer entertainment for those who came week by week. We just gave them God and He satisfied their every need and ignited a desire for more of Him but it took a while to get to this place.

When we started the group we inherited what had been a typical youth club ethos. We would have table tennis and board games available for the first part of the evening and then we would have the 'religious' bit. But this was not working at all. I remember the moment of crisis and the revelation that changed everything.

I was locking up late one night after the Youth meeting and I was alone. I'd put all the things away myself and was rather disappointed and felt sorry for myself and confused. No one seemed a bit interested in Jesus and I was complaining to God as I turned the key to lock the front door of the Church Hall. I looked up at the dark star studded sky.

"Lord," I shouted angrily, "when are they going to show the slightest bit of interest in You. I've earnestly prayed for them all and I've believed for them to get saved but there is no change. What more can I do?"

Suddenly the Lord spoke back, "Howard. It's not what you do for me that blesses me but it's you and your love for Me. And I too want to love you. Let go and let me do it and see what will happen." At that very moment I realised that all this time I had been striving to prove my worth to God and gain His favour and to earn His love.

I knew then that only God the eternal Spirit could create changes of eternal spiritual significance. I let go and surrendered to Him and His will. The next week I had decided to forget the games and the entertainment and instead had invited an evangelist friend to come along and speak and simply share the gospel message of salvation. I had during the week remembered what Rev. David Wilkerson of Teen Challenge Centre and of the book 'The Cross and the Switchblade' said when he was asked how he got the street gang kids of New York interested in God, and he said, "I don't give them games and I don't give them religion. I give them God and His power and His love and they can't have enough of it."

All we did that night was to let the visitor speak for about thirty minutes and afterward he made an appeal for those present to show their willingness to accept salvation by raising their hands. Over thirty teenagers responded and we spent the rest of the evening leading them to Jesus through repentance and faith. Zechariah 4:6 "This is the word of the Lord to Zerubbabel: 'Not by might, nor by power, but by my Spirit,' says the Lord Almighty."

From that night onwards these 70 teenagers began to gather together each week hungry for more and more of God and His Word and because of my friendship and ministry involvement with many leaders of the Charismatic and the new House Church Movement here in England, these young people received so much precious impartation from many of the front line Christian leaders of the day. Soon they were all filled with the Spirit and spoke in tongues and we witnessed many signs and wonders and miracles as God moved amongst us. It was a wonderful season and it lasted until we moved away from London and down to Cornwall in the far southwest of England.

Really the CYFA Youth Group existed separately from the rather traditional St. Giles Church of England and its liberal churchmanship. I think the young people would have proved too hot for them to handle. But there was a growing number of adult communicants at St Giles that had expressed a desire for a deeper experience of God, so when a friend of ours from Hampshire, a Canon in the Anglican Church, the Right Rev. Canon Wallace Byrd who was part of the Renewal Movement in England, arranged a Service of Worship and Renewal at the Cathedral of the Holy Spirit in Guildford, I booked a large coach and took a group of rather unsuspecting Anglicans (i.e. from the Church of England) from St. Giles'

Parish to experience the power of Holy Spirit at work in His Church.

When we arrived it was just about to start and we were ushered in to an over- crowded cathedral that was buzzing with expectation. The flow of the Spirit, the dancing, the flags, the soaring of singing in tongues, was simply awesome. At times God's Holy Presence was demonstrated by a depth of silence and stillness only to be compared in the earthly realm to a sense of diving into a dark pool of deep pure fresh water where after the initial plunge every sound is suddenly silenced and you are totally embraced by silence.

The two hour Cathedral service was over too soon and our Anglican friends, now back on the coach, sat perhaps a little bemused trying to process what they had just experienced. I overheard one of the conversations as I walked up the aisle checking on passengers. I hovered around looking at my clipboard but listening to them talking about the beautiful singing.

"Wasn't that wonderful? I felt so invigorated by it all," they said. "And the choirs. Wow! They must have rehearsed for hours. They were so together and all without a conductor. How did they know when to start and when to stop? And I loved the harmonies, in thirds and fifths and octaves. Oh, so so beautiful."

I laughed to myself. They were simply referencing the congregation singing in tongues. "Would life at St Giles Church ever be the same again?" I thought. Although we were in Hillingdon for six years altogether, it was only a few months after being married and arriving there that we fostered a young man of sixteen called Melvin who was a pupil at Townmead School. He became a dear son to us and now loves the Lord Jesus and lives and serves Him up in Lincolnshire, England. Then after four years our daughter and first born, Rachael, was born and joined the family and two years later, Jon.

Tricia, who had left Secondary School teaching a year after our marriage, had had a lovely time teaching 8 and 9 year olds at Pinkwell Junior School, Hayes, Middlesex until Rachael was born in 1971. It was a great time of healing for Tricia after the traumatic first teaching post she had at Townmead.

As that school summer break of 1972 approached we decided to take a well- earned holiday in a place we had holidayed before and of which we had such good memories. And so with much anticipation we booked an apartment in the beautiful seaside town of Fowey in Cornwall on the far South West coast of England and began to prepare. What a significant decision this was to prove to be. It was the experience that transitioned us into the next stage of our personal journey towards our Bridegroom.

Proverbs 3:6 "in all your ways acknowledge him and he will make your paths straight."

Chapter 7: The Call to Cornwall

"Go down to Cornwall and join my people and stand against the enemy".

The LORD says, "I will instruct you and teach you in the way you should go; I will counsel you and watch over you." Psalm 32:8.

It was not just 'any' holiday to Cornwall but it was a special holiday that would change everything. It was a part of a much bigger journey that we were on. This holiday would result in a new season, a new place to live in, a new school, a new church family and eventually an amazing fresh revelation that would eventually release a new mandate.

The holiday was so refreshing and relaxing. It's such a beautiful part of England. When I now describe Cornwall to someone I do so in five words all beginning with the letter 'S'. Sea, Sun, Sand, Surf and Sail. It's the farthest county west of London and if you picture the map of the United Kingdom and imagine it as in the shape of a man's foot with his big toe pointing to the left then Cornwall is in the big toe. So there is sea on the northern and southern coasts and sea around the farthest western tip which is famously known as Land's End. It's a land of Celtic origin, famous Cornish pasties which are hand held, crescent shaped, meat and vegetable pies and a land of quaint coves and fishing villages.

Tricia and myself and little Rachael stayed for this holiday in the very typical Cornish fishing village of Fowey near St

Austell with its narrow roads bedecked with colourful bunting and the one way traffic system through the town that wound its way along the main shopping street parallel to the Fowey River. We were blessed on Sunday by a wonderful morning service held at the evangelical Anglican Church right in the centre of town. Throughout the week we visited as much of the coastline around as we could and soon found ourselves wishing we lived there.

We beached and swam and walked. We really didn't want to return to our home and caught ourselves looking in housing agents' shop windows to see the prices of property in Cornwall. We actually felt we belonged there. It was strange thinking of leaving. Was it just a case of holiday fever? Many I'm told catch the same disease whilst there. But after returning home to Hillingdon on the west side of London, the longing to be in Cornwall again persisted and in fact grew stronger.

Some months later in the February half-term holiday of the following school year we decided that maybe God was indeed leading us to move somewhere new and that we would return to Cornwall again but this time in the middle of winter when the skies were grey and the Cornish wind and rain would dismiss any false romantic notions or remains of 'holiday fever'. Against these odds only the certainty of God's call would make us pick up sticks and relocate. So that February we left Hillingdon once again to make the long journey to the far south western shores of England.

'Testing the Spirit' to know God's will in all matters is so important but Father helped us by sending us really bad weather during the whole of our visit which enabled us to assess our feelings for this place more accurately. Wow! It didn't stop raining the whole journey and the whole time we were there. The rain was coming down in bucket loads and "Dear of 'im'", as they say there in Cornwall. It was 'proper job' and 'blowing a real hooley'.

And there was more. The flat we had booked had a flies nest in every bay window. Rachael who was at the stage of only shuffling along on her bottom got splinters in that rear tender end and the whole flat was cold and damp. Nevertheless the feeling of belonging remained strong and we returned to Hillingdon confident that God was calling us to pastures new.

We had His witness in our spirit. This was the first witness. The Bible talks about things being affirmed and confirmed by the mouth of two or three witnesses so we prayed that God would honour his word and do just that. 2 Corinthians 13:1.

Several days later Tricia had a Word from the Lord, an instruction, no, a command. It was, "Go down to Cornwall, join my people and stand against the enemy." We were both unsure as to what that meant but sensed it was something to do with intercession and spiritual warfare. Later we learnt that Cornwall was and is a stronghold of Druidism and ancient witchcraft and other secret societies.

But if that was the second 'witness' where was the third? Scripture did say two or three and I suppose I wanted three. So I decided to write to some Christians friends in Cornwall who I had recently got to know and share Tricia's Word with them. To my joy and surprise they immediately wrote back welcoming us to Cornwall and telling us that that message from the Lord was exactly the same message word for word that the Lord had given to them when they came down to the county some years earlier. We had received our three witnesses.

We were now assured that we were in the will of God so I decided I would work out my contract at the current school and then hand my notice in. During the next six weeks' summer holiday we packed up our things and moved in September to a land which was the furthest south west of London we could go, to live and serve and to "join His people."

But God is extravagant with His love blessing because he provided a fourth witness to confirm His will, even more so. Although it was for a mission that we were going to Cornwall I was going to go in through the teaching gate, as it were, in order to provide for my family so I needed a job. Now in those days Cornwall was quite parochial and jobs it seemed were shared around within the county, especially teaching jobs.

I looked regularly in the national Times Educational Supplement at teaching vacancies but nothing for Cornwall ever seemed to appear. Months went by and I needed to give my notice but still nothing in Cornwall schools was being advertised. I even wrote to the County Education Office in Truro to ask for the county teaching vacancy list but there were no vacancies for my subject advertised there either. It was perhaps because there were no job vacancies or they got filled within the county before they were ever advertised.

Feeling a little confused that day I went to take a break in the school staff room as I had a free teaching period and there sat a more senior teacher than myself who had recently joined the staff but all I knew about her was that she was a professional friend of the headmaster and was biding her time at the school filling in for any absent teachers.

We started talking and I mentioned that I was thinking of leaving that summer to live and teach in Cornwall but that I couldn't find any jobs there. Nothing ever seemed to be advertised in the Times Educational Supplement, especially for Head of RE in any Cornish schools.

"Oh are you the Head of RE here? I'm pleased to meet you. I'm an RE teacher too and have headed up several RE departments in the past but I'm just biding my time waiting for any appointment that comes along. Cornwall you say? Have you not seen this week's Times Educational Supplement. There is a Head of RE post advertised for Penryn School near Falmouth in Cornwall. I thought about it myself but it's too far away for me. Why don't you apply?" So, in one stroke God had provided a job for both of us, providing of course we both passed the interviews. I took this again as another witness. God was being so extravagant!

I did apply and so did she and in due time we both took up our new appointments, hers in my place at Barnhill School, Hayes, Middlesex and mine at Penryn School near the seaside town of Falmouth in Cornwall. I came for my interview and on the same day as I was offered the job, bought a three bedroom bungalow close to the school and returned to Tricia in Middlesex, to tell her the good news. Surely God does all things well.

Psalm 145:9 "The LORD is good to all; he has compassion on all he has made."

Chapter 8: Brass Band Music is the Music of Heaven

Psalm 150:3 "Praise him with the sounding of the trumpet; praise him with the harp and lyre."

My grandfather always used to say that when all the believers march into heaven at the end of the age the Salvation Army Band will be leading the way. I'm not sure about this presumption nor his eschatology or theology.

However, like him, I too love brass band music and brass bands and this ability to play brass instruments was to provide, later on, a new opportunity for me to teach brass in schools. Tricia and I soon settled into life in Penryn Town and myself into the new School. However teaching RE in 1973 was so different to how it is today. Today of course it is based on a study of the major world religions, but then it was all about Christianity and the study of key books of the Bible.

I could reinforce the lessons on Christianity by bringing in Christians who had an amazing testimony and experience of Jesus and the Christian faith. Consequently my classroom saw many visitors taking or sharing the lessons, whether they were local Pastors or nationally well-known Christian personalities, or gospel singers, performers or a Christian Gospel band. When Gospel Singing Groups came in they would perform in the school Religious Assemblies first thing in the morning, and then they divided up so each member could join a class and share their story. At lunchtime or after school pupils could attend a full Gospel concert.

The highlight one year for me was the visit to Cornwall of the ex. New York gang leader and now Christian preacher Nicky Cruz of the books The Cross and the Switchblade and Run Baby Run fame. He was speaking at the large auditorium at Carlyon Bay, Cornwall, for several nights. I had already read these books to most of the senior pupils in their RE lessons and showed most of the school the film version of The Cross and the Switchblade, so when I advertised the event so many pupils wanted to come that I had to hire three double decker buses to transport them all. Many, many pupils surrendered their lives to Jesus that night and our School Christian Union meetings tripled in size.

At the beginning of the school year in 1976 I became aware that the Lord was troubling me about something that He wanted me to consider doing in school. RE was changing in the UK to reflect our more multi-religious and multi-cultural society. Interest in religion and particularly in Christianity within the UK was also diminishing for many. I had become concerned as to how I might present a more relevant image of myself as a Christian and as an RE teacher to the pupils in a changing society where liberalism and humanism were gaining favour.

I wouldn't compromise my faith or testimony as a believer but I wanted another way to relate to pupils other than just as an RE teacher. RE teachers, especially Christian RE teachers, represented in the minds of an increasing number of pupils a particular type of person and consequently

Christianity wasn't for everybody. I wanted them to realise that believing in God and knowing Him and His Son Jesus was the most exciting experience anyone could ever have. I was looking around for some other school activity I could get involved in that might help that cause.

One day as I was walking into school from the music room entrance I heard some very strange sounds coming from a classroom. It was from a small group of pupils who were being tutored by the Head of Music to make some sounds from a rather battered set of brass instruments. Poking my head around the door I apologised for any interruption but asked if I might help and explained that I played brass instruments myself since I had a Salvation Army background. And that's how it all started.

The favour of God was on this move and soon I had formed a small brass band. It took a lot of my time but I loved training the pupils and the band members were so committed and practised so hard. We experienced so much success and I continued training them until eventually we had three Brass Bands, one from pupils from the first two years of the school and the second from senior pupils and later a senior band called Saracen Brass which was open to all pupils and even those that had left school, but on the basis of ability. We were soon taking many engagements as did the junior school's band too. We also enjoyed competing in Brass Band competitions and Music Festivals. Yet even upon this activity God breathed His Spirit and many band members got saved.

The practice of praying for the school early each day was something I had always been led to do. I met with a local evangelist at 8am each morning to pray for the school in general, the Christian Union and the members of the brass bands. God's blessing became so evident because I remember driving the school's 35 seater coach packed full of music stands, pupils and instruments to a Saturday engagement. All of the band members sang Christian worship songs and choruses as we travelled to the venue. Most had become Christians.

Yes we worked very hard and practised together for long hours but God favoured us and in 1981 we won through to take part in the National Festival of Music for Youth at the Royal Festival Hall, London and then on four more subsequent occasions. I also remember driving the same coach myself all the way to London and back, a distance of over 600 miles (over 965 km), in order to perform at that music festival. During those visits we gained several 'Highly Commended' awards and were second only to Wardle High School Band (now Wardle Academy) who were then and still are the feeder band for the famous Championship Black Dyke Mills Brass Band from the north of England.

We would rehearse somewhere in London before finally going to the festival and I remember doing so on one occasion in the Royal Ballet School's dance studio beside the Royal Albert Hall. It was amazing to see the pupils rehearsing the classic piece for the organ, 'Suite Gothique' which had been wonderfully transcribed for brass band and to hear those powerful full chords echoing through those hallowed corridors. Another time I remember performing a concert by invitation in Covent Garden outside the Royal Opera Theatre, and then another time on the Band Stand in the famous Hyde Park, London.

During that period of about eleven years the Band appeared several times on Westwood Television and Radio Cornwall. We made several CD's and took Band Tours to Europe, including Audierne, France (the French town with whom Penryn was twinned) and Berlin in Germany.

I remember our tour in Germany so well. We stayed in the old Olympic stadium and rehearsed there on the very spot where Hitler stood and from where he watched the games and presented the medals. We lodged in the athletes' old changing rooms so one of the band members may well have stayed in the one Jesse Jackson had used.

The highlight of that tour was when we gave a concert in the Europa Strasse in the middle of Berlin and played Queen's Bohemian Rhapsody for Brass to tumultuous applause, only to hear afterwards that Queen themselves had performed this famous piece on the same spot the week earlier. Even though these were quite different activities to those like the School Christian Union Club and could be considered 'secular', we always prayed over any decisions and sought His pleasure and favour.

As my involvement in brass in the school increased, several of my Christian brothers and sisters and local leaders felt, I'm sure, concerned about my priorities. But I knew it was all for Him and a means of training children in commitment, determination, discipline and that as it is for our Jewish brothers, God makes no distinction between the secular and the religious.

I was so blessed when one of my Christian friends took the time and trouble to come down to the bandstand at Falmouth's Council Gardens, called The Princess Pavilion, to hear us give a Sunday afternoon concert. We always played several hymns as part of our programme and I took the opportunity to share a brief Word about the hymn and its meaning. God knew my heart. I did not know that this friend of mine was in the audience but afterwards he wrote to me and said, "Howard, I really felt the Holy Spirit's presence and the anointing on the playing today. It was very moving. I was so blessed. Thank you."

However in 1987 I felt the Lord wanted me to close the Senior Band down after eleven years and phase out the school bands too unless someone else could be found to pick up the baton, literally. We had a marvellous run. We had won the School Brass Band Music Festival in Cornwall repeatedly for many years, moved up the Senior Sections of the Cornwall Brass Band Association, played at the opening of Radio Cornwall, gave a concert by invitation on Paddington Railway Station, London, to celebrate the opening of the Great Western Railway service from London to Cornwall in 1996 and had the privilege of playing for Prince Charles and Diana at an event they opened in Cornwall. We also had the honour of accompanying Dame Vera Lynn in concert singing 'The White Cliffs of Dover during her visit to a major event in the county.

Our final band tour would have been the 'icing on the cake' of a great musical 'season' for us but the proposed and much planned tour of China that we were about to begin was suddenly aborted. We would have been the first brass band in the world to have given a concert tour of China since the communist revolution that closed the doors to such foreign visits for many years. However what happened is quite amazing and although the tour never took place, the events leading up to our proposed departure date were quite incredible.

It came about in the first place as a convergence between two ideas. One was to take part in the Hong Kong Music Festival the following year since we had already been successful at our own UK one several times. I had already received an invitation for the band to play at the Hong Kong festival on the strength of this. The second idea was to solicit an invitation from the Youth Department of the Chinese Government to visit China and give a joint concert with the Chinese National Youth Choir at several of China's premier concert halls and universities.

I didn't even know if they had a National Youth Choir but I knew that if they were interested in such a tour then they would have created one. China was looking for opportunities to develop overseas relationships and trade agreements. It was the right time. Originally the idea was to tour Hong Kong and go into China for just two days for one concert but before I actually wrote the letter the whole idea had morphed and the tour had reversed and become a week's concert tour of China and then a stop off in Hong Kong on the way back to the UK to take part in their Music Festival.

So my letter was written and posted. I knew this would be a very attractive proposal to them because I suggested that if this went ahead we would reciprocate by inviting the Youth Choir of China to London to hold a joint concert in the prestigious Royal Albert Hall. I knew an entrepreneur from Cornwall who could arrange that as he had recently arranged a very successful and financially profitable concert for massed Cornish Male Voice Choirs there.

I sent a letter to the Chinese attache in London which was passed on to the correct personnel to deal with it and so correspondence began. Somehow Lord Belstead at our Foreign Office in London got to hear sometime later about these negotiations and wrote to me offering to send all my correspondence out to China via the 'diplomatic bag' as it would guarantee the arrival of my letters but this was probably as much for national security reasons as much as it was a generous offer.

Months went by and I heard nothing. I had informed our school secretarial staff that a letter might be coming sometime from China for me and please send it to me in my class room. But time went by. Then one morning a child arrived in my RE room with a letter which had a postmark from China. It was from the People's Republic of China and the Minister of Youth Affairs. It contained that invitation. The tour was to begin in Peking and follow a programme of a number of concerts in China's conservatories of music and major concert halls. We agreed to call it 'From Penryn to Peking'.

Lord Belstead was not the only person to hear about it but Boosey and Hawkes the music publishers and instrument makers did too and wrote to me offering to sponsor this tour since they had been trying to arrange a similar tour for one of our UK military bands but because of the military nature of the band and our delicate sensitive relationships still with China they suggested that they abort that sponsorship and offered it to us. The consequence of this was that the band received a brand new set of premier brass instruments and travelled to Boosey's London factory some time later to receive them.

This sponsorship attracted others to follow suit. Yorkshire Television Company were going to make a documentary about the trip and Cathy Pacific Airline were offering us half price airfares for agreed publicity through the tour brochures and TV film and finally Wimpey International in partnership with Wimpey Homes, a huge UK building company, offered their sponsorship too.

At that time many UK trade fairs were travelling to China made up of consortiums of various British companies hoping to gain trade agreements with this fast developing nation. Everything was coming together amazingly well and as the band practices increased to three nights a week, the quality of their playing was just amazing. We were so proud of them. There was a real sense of excitement about the forth- coming tour but then the bomb was dropped.

The UK government put out a memo to all British companies that were sponsoring any foreign trade fairs, sports tours or musical events warning them that China was welcoming these events but so far was not responding with any trade agreements. They were observing and studying the new initiatives, inventions or manufacturing and technical developments and gathering much knowledge but not offering any trade contracts. The advice from the government was to close down all sponsorships. Over-night the sponsorship bubble burst and our major supporters withdrew. The tour had to be aborted three months before departure. In many ways it heralded for me the end of the brass band period of my life and I felt intuitively that a new season was about to begin.

Actually, music was not my subject and this was all done voluntarily and the growing pressure for better examination results in all school subjects was increasing and was at times overbearing. I needed to re-evaluate the use of my time and concentrate more on what I was being paid to do as an RE and Social Education teacher in the school.

In addition to teaching RE I had been busy developing a course of Social and Personal Education, a non-examination subject for every pupil in the school, which covered issues of life such as Careers Education, Health Education, Political Education, Financial and Economic Education, Relationship Developments, and Road Safety Awareness. I was blessed to receive the Prince Michael National Award for Road Safety Awareness in Schools and enjoyed a reception at the Savoy Hotel in London where I was presented with it.

But no success measured up to that experience of seeing the influence that the band training had had upon the band member's lives, some of whom would have gone astray without that sense of belonging and the regular discipline of rehearsals. It was indeed a golden period in my teaching career but it had to come to an end and now He said it was time to move on.

However since then some have asked me if I was disappointed about not going to China or Hong Kong and whether I missed the band and its music and my answer was always the same. "I'm so grateful to Father for that wonderful experience but when God calls you to do something, He enables you. God gave me the grace to do it for all those years and then to announce its closure and to step down and away from the life that had at times almost consumed me." The Bible says that the Lord gives and the Lord takes away. Blessed be the name of the Lord. Job 1:21, and He knows what is best.

Chapter 9: Success and the Self-Made Man

"Do not love the world or anything in the world. If anyone loves the world, the love of the Father is not in him. For all that is in the world—the cravings of sinful man, the lust of his eyes and the boasting of what he has and does—comes not from the Father but from the world." 1 John 2:15-16.

I finally finished with the Band and immersed myself only in classroom teaching and concentrated on the new type of RE that had evolved, reinventing myself. I had prepared myself for these changed and had studied the five major world religions so I could teach about them with some degree of confidence. There were many new courses and many meetings to attend. Accountability and line management were the 'in' words and a reality too. No longer was a teacher a king of his own castle and relatively unaccountable but was now under intense scrutiny, extremely accountable, part of a team and if a head of a growing department as I was, then was also involved in developing departmental training and producing regular reports for the school's senior management. But the Lord walked through it all with me.

I sensed strongly that what lay ahead of me was something very different from what I had done before. There were going to be uncomfortable and challenging things to learn about myself, who I was and about what God was calling me to do and be. In many ways it was a very unsettling time because everything seemed to be altering with the goal posts changing regularly. Things internally and spiritually were also under examination in my life but from the Lord Himself and He never leaves a stone unturned.

For me it was a time of deep heart searching and questioning, particularly about who I was. I was not Mr Barnes, the Brass Band man any more, nor Mr Barnes the RE Teacher and really I never ever was in God's eyes. These were the jobs I did or roles I played. They didn't define who I was, inside and especially in relation to the Father. It was a challenging time of self- evaluation and of discovering my own unique identity.

It was quite a dark time in my life though. I was in a place I'd never been before and I knew that this journey I was on was not towards 'somewhere' but towards 'someone'. My journey toward the Bridegroom was intensifying. There is always a wilderness experience in our walk with the Lord and sometimes even more than one experience. In fact, in Hosea 2:14, Father God even seems to promise such an experience: Therefore I am now going to allure her; I will lead her into the desert," but what so many miss is the next part, "and speak tenderly to her."

For it is in the wilderness that He can get our attention. The world is a very noisy place. There are so many voices competing for our ears and our minds and hearts. But when these are quietened or even shut out then His voice can be heard above the tumult or in the silence. There is a secret place we can go, where we can hear the "still small voice of calm".

It has been said that God shouts His truths but whispers His secrets? Scripture tells us that the "heavens declare the glory of God" Psalm 19:1. His creative ability and artistry is made so evident by the glory of the heavens. These things shout out about His glory so loudly. But He shares the deeper and more intimate things about Himself and the secrets of His heart as if in whispers and only those close enough to Him can hear them.

All those who will hear the voice of God intimately must go through their wilderness experience for it is here amidst the confusion, loss of personal identity or the sight of His face, that the pruning and re-examination and transformation takes place. Painful though this time is, it is a positive and not a negative experience. Moses knew that experience. So did Elijah and John the Baptist and even Jesus Himself.

But remember that the wilderness is NOT the place of God's judgement or of punishment but it is the place of romance. He wants to romance our heart. Oh how He longs to do that and to draw us to Himself.

St John of the Cross calls this experience the 'dark night of the soul' but let us all remember that the light always shines brightest in the darkest place. It ever was so. Isaiah 9:2 "The people walking in darkness have seen a great light; on those living in the land of the shadow of death a light has dawned."

I had given up the Brass band and I was reinventing myself in terms of teaching multi religions, something I hadn't entered the teaching profession for, but I was also disillusioned with the way Health Education was being influenced by non- Christian ethics and new attitudes about gender, sexuality and marriage. It was still the early years of the new millennium (2000's) but the signs of rapid change were clear to be seen. The course in Social Education and Personal Development for all pupils that I had developed over twenty or more years was now being influenced towards liberalism, humanism and the acceptance of same sex marriage relationships. Nothing was the same anymore.

But beneath all this was lurking the real issue. It wasn't about these things really. It was about me and who I was and my relationship with the Lord. Despite the fact that I had known Him as my Saviour since I was eight years of age and I did indeed have many testimonies of His power, healing and presence in my life, I was very much still a self-made child of God. Yes, I was someone saved by His sacrifice on the cross, cleansed by His blood, certainly. But someone who knew how to spend time in His presence? No, definitely not.

I knew about the importance of prayer. All the miracles, salvations and moves of God I had seen over the years were born out of prayer. But this praying was all done in the company of others. I found prayer on my own difficult. When I prayed on my own it was to ask Him for things. I sought His hands only. My prayers reflected this. I wanted His provision. I wanted His 'handouts'. I sought Him for my needs to be met and sometimes my prayers were more like a shopping list of things to get than a real prayer. My prayers were all about MY needs and not His. I knew little about His needs.

In fact I knew little of His ways. Yes like Moses I knew His 'Acts' in my life but knew little of his intimate ways. Moses cried out for that and I knew deep down inside I wanted to know that too. But first the situation I was in was going to get even worse. As this period continued everything seemed to go very wrong in my life and in every area of it. I don't want to go into detail but as a result I nearly lost my marriage, my family, my job, my ministry at the church.

At school, I was put under full disciplinary action by the new Headteacher for something I'd not done and for which I was eventually cleared by the intervention of the National President of the National Union of Teachers. It was an awful time and it broke me. I remember crying out to the Lord in my pain saying, "Lord, I don't know who I am anymore!" His answer was blunt but reassuring. "I know. But that's why I've allowed it. Up till now you have been a product of your own creation. Now I can mould you and transform you into the person I always planned for you to be even before the foundations of the earth. Now may I show you who you really are?"

During my last three years at Penryn School, a woman with a powerful prophetic ministry came to stay with Tricia and myself whilst she sought the Lord about where she should go next. She was an Intercessor and spent the days of her widowhood travelling around England stopping off at places of past Revivals in order to pray at these old wells to see them reopen. There had been a wonderful move of God in Cornwall in times past and she was here under His instruction to pray for a renewal of that same Holy Spirit.

One day she told me that God had given her my 'spiritual name'. Wow. I was so blessed and intrigued and asked her to share it with me. "No," she said. "You must seek the Lord for it yourself, on your own, and when He tells you then you tell me and I'll show you my diary for this day and you will see whether you are right." "Ouch! That's tough. How do I seek God like that?" I said to myself. But it was the best thing she could have done for me.

I really tried to listen to Him but it took several months and a lot of discipline. Yet about three months later He spoke to me and gave me a long name that was in the Old Testament which I had to look up. But I couldn't forget it because He had impressed it deeply into my spirit. I sensed this was the name. As I researched about it I found that it had a very significant meaning and the person who was called by it had a wonderful role and calling to fulfil.

So now being sure I had found it, I ran quickly to her and said that I believed the Father had heard my prayer and had given me a name which may be my 'spiritual name' and could she look at her diary? She found the entry and showed me the place where she had written down, some four months previously, a biblical name and its Bible reference. It was the same name.

I had heard His voice and had begun at last to hear Him speak clearly to me. I knew now that hearing His voice was going to be the most precious thing I could experience. Any success in ministry would depend on it. The name God gave me was personal to me and not necessarily something to be shared publicly here and I don't feel I have His permission to reveal it but enough to say that the role I now fulfil in the ministry of Call2Come around the world is so very consistent with the role that this Old Testament figure fulfilled.

It was after this prophetic intercessor left our home and moved up to pray in the Hebridean Islands that He used her once again to help me to learn to 'seek His face' more intensely. One day she wrote to me from Scotland with a scripture that challenged me to the core.

You see, that morning in my brief prayer time, I had received Psalm 27:8 from the Lord: "You have said, 'Seek My face [inquire for and require My presence as your vital need]' and my heart says to you, 'Your face (Your presence), Lord, will I seek'" (Amplified Version). I was so stirred by this verse and was considering how I needed to respond to it when a letter arrived from our intercessor friend. It contained a brief message stating that the Lord had spoken to her and given her a verse for me and it was imperative that I acted on it. It was exactly the same verse. Psalm 27:8.

So from that moment onwards I committed myself to get up at 5 am every morning and to seek Him for two hours each day. I would also fast as He led me and I promised that I would never look back. I was excited about what would happen as a result and eagerly waited for the next day for those early hours of the morning when I would begin my vigil.

I mentioned previously that seeking God's face was essential if we were to experience any success in our Christian life. However I'd like to say a little more about the word success because I've come to understand that God does not evaluate success in the way we do. I was thinking one day about the successful times I had had in the various schools I had been privileged to serve in over the years and thanking the Lord for such an opportunity when He interrupted my train of thought by saying "I don't want you to use the word success. It's because the world today has devalued and corrupted it".

The Lord showed me that many people even in His Church base their assessment of what is successful upon the size of a congregation, the amount of money in the tithes or gifts, the size of the Pastor's car or house. But prosperity does not indicate the degree of your success. They will say "Oh the Pastor must be successful because God has blessed him with a new car." Even in the area of personal ministry witnessing or prayer, success is often measured in terms of how many people have been witnessed to or led to find Christ as their Saviour. "So, No. I don't want you to be successful" He said again, "At least not in the way the world would evaluate it. But I do want you to be 'Eternally Significant!'

One day when all is revealed and our Father has sorted out the gold from the 'wood, hay and stubble' we will then know what He considers to be successful. Only those things that are of eternal significance will receive His "Well done!" and if there are any crowns to be given out, our only response should be to cast them all down at His feet, This following story explains what true success is in His eyes.

A friend of mine was given a vision and in this vision he was taken to heaven and found himself in the outer court. It was full of glorious light and it stunned his eyes so that he could not see. As he got used to the brilliance he began to make out the outline of others who were there and he thought he recognised one or two as Christian people of some notoriety and success in ministry in times past. It was good to see them there but one thing troubled him. Why were they there in the outer court and not in the inner court nearest to the throne room?

His curiosity to know the answer drove him to approach one individual whom he was sure he recognised and ask a little nervously, "Excuse me. Sorry to disturb you but aren't you that great hymn writer of times past? Thank you for your wonderful contribution to our Christian heritage. You have blessed me so much with your inspirational words. But I'm a little confused. Why are you here in this outer court and not at least in the inner chamber?" The hymn writer looked down for a moment and then up at me. "I am so grateful even to be here for I deserve nothing. It's all by His grace. But you see, I loved my hymn writing more than I loved Him and I took pride in my ability to create verses."

He smiled at me and moved on.

Then I found myself in the inner court and this time the radiance and light was even more glorious. It took far longer this time to adjust my eyes to the glare but as they did once again I found I could make out more people and indeed more people of Christian history that I recognised. A young woman was moving my way and yes it was her. I knew her immediately. She had been a famous Worship Leader and had such a beautiful voice. She had blessed so many with her singing of worship songs. She was the well- known worship leader I had listened to at a Concert in my youth. Tragically she had been prematurely killed in a road accident whilst travelling to a huge worship event some time ago now.

But why was she here? Thousands had come to Christ through her concerts! I didn't understand.

After a short while I introduced myself and asked her why she was there and not in the Throne Room.

"Oh indeed I loved singing for my Lord but gradually the attention and adulation I received began to become more important than the Lord Himself. But I'm so grateful to be even here. It's by His grace."

Finally, I found myself in that Throne Room and was simply not prepared for the intensity of light that shone there. It was a strange but beautiful light, a vibrating healing light like warm liquid gold intermingled with multiple reflections of iridescent colours of known and unknown hues. My eyes would never fully accommodate this vibrant and all-embracing light.

Eventually I was able to see just the shape of a person silhouetted against what was like a golden throne. I knew it was HIS throne. The person was kneeling there, her shadowy form leaning against the glorious translucent frame of the one who was known as the Alpha and Omega, the Bright and Morning Star, the Lamb of God, the Lion of Judah, the Lover of our souls. I could just make out that she was kneeling there gazing up into His face. I felt embarrassed as if I had entered a bridal chamber and had interrupted a moment of the most pure and perfect intimacy.

Who was this person? What great act of great service had she rendered or ministry established when on earth? What position had she held or ecclesial accolades received? I was so intrigued to know who she was because, I didn't recognise her. Eventually my curiosity was too much and while she rearranged her position a little I bent forward and whispered,

"Hello. Please forgive me for asking but, Who are you? I don't know you. You must have been someone so, so special."

"Oh no. You will never have heard of me. I'm very insignificant in your world's eyes."

"But you must have been a famous Christian singer?" I said.

"Ha ha, oh no. If you heard my voice you would not say that."

"Then you must have written many books"

"I'm illiterate. I've never been to school."

"Well then, please tell me. What did you do to merit this position of sitting at His feet? What is your name and who are you?"

Slowly she turned towards me and looked deep into my eyes. I felt I could see so much pain etched there and travail of soul poured out during many dark and long nights of prayer.

Then she began to answer my question to tell me who she was and as she did she turned towards Him once again and lifting a finger pointed at His face saying, "I am HIS. That's who I am."

2ion score

Our true identity and significance, our success or value, must be in loving Him and found in Him alone.

A Journey of Ascent Towards the Bridegroom

Chapter 10: Time Travel

"Philip, however, appeared at Azotus, and travelled about, preaching the gospel in all the towns until he reached Caesarea." Acts 8:40

"I tell you the truth, anyone who has faith in me will do what I have been doing. He will do even greater things than these, because I am going to the Father. And I will do whatever you ask in my name, so that the Son may bring glory to the Father. You may ask me for anything in my name, and I will do it." John 14:12 –14.

"I am the LORD; that is my name! I will not give my glory to another or my praise to idols." Isaiah 42:8

As I continued to learn more about how to seek His face and to recognise His voice, my spiritual antennae seemed to become far more sensitive and my hunger for Him intensified. I was far more aware of the spiritual realm than ever before in my life and God began to encourage the spiritual gifts of Discernment of Spirits or of the Word of Knowledge or Wisdom to develop and to be used in a growing number of counselling situations that seemed to present themselves. People would get healed or delivered more regularly in answer to prayer. In fact it was a season of seeing many wonderful miracles and 'signs and wonders'.

I share here the following experience that I had, not only to encourage faith within the Bride, but also to expose the weakness of human personality and our vulnerability and that of my own, from which God protected me. I also do so to illustrate the amazing grace of God and to underline that if as the Bride we are being transformed to be totally compatible with our Bridegroom then everything is possible to us, even now.

The scripture found in Acts 8:40 about Philip being 'translated' from where he was ministering to the Ethiopian Eunuch to Azotus has fascinated believers and cynics alike. The Old Testament records the stories of several people being translated, people like Enoch and Elijah. In their case they were transported to heaven. It appears that Jesus especially in His resurrected body also experienced this spiritual phenomena and possibly in His ministry before His resurrection as when He appeared walking on the water in the middle of the Sea of Galilee. How did He get there? See Matthew 14:22-33. If He is the 'plumb line' against which we compare our own life and ministry then when we see Him disappearing and appearing somewhere else at will maybe we should expect to experience the same in our ministry whenever God requires it.

Certainly in His resurrected body we know that Jesus moved freely between the realm of natural earth's space and time and that of the eternal, spiritual realm. He appeared on the beach in Galilee and offered the disciples breakfast. He walked through the walls into the room in Jerusalem and He was physically translated at His ascension.

I too had such an experience which is so difficult to rationalise.

Towards the end of the season in my life whilst I was still teaching in Penryn School in Cornwall, UK, I had a most amazing experience. It was a time when I was also quite active in Christian youth work within the local Churches where I lived. Often this work would include counselling and prayer sessions with people in my home which would be with Tricia my wife or at least under her covering especially if it was a woman.

One time I was ministering to a young lady and was sensing the wisdom and guidance of the Holy Spirit but I was also conscious that I needed to draw the session to a close because I had another meeting that evening, a few miles away, at a church youth group that had been recently touched by a move of the Spirit. The temptation was to get stressed because I needed to close this first meeting appropriately and then travel to the church.

Time just seemed to evaporate and I was already very late for the second appointment. The young lady eventually left and I got ready to go knowing clearly that I simply hadn't time to travel the distance and arrive before the meeting was scheduled to begin. Yet in my heart I knew He was aware of this and had not allowed me to leave any earlier. Every time I questioned what to do in my mind whilst counselling the young woman the Lord had assured me that it would alright.

So now that I was ready I decided to begin my journey and trust Him.

As I started to walk away from my house and opened the gate to the road, I actually found myself opening the gate to the small path up to the church main door. But how I got there I have no idea. I was neither flustered nor out of breath and my spirit was fully prepared to share what He had given me to say. I must have been translated. That was a miracle of supernatural quality but the other miracle, equally as great, was that from that day on and for thirty years after I totally forgot about that experience and so never ever shared it with anyone. So how is it that I have remembered it now and can share it here?

Well, some thirty year later I was speaking at a church fellowship meeting in my area and afterwards a woman in her fifties came to me and introduced herself as someone who was in that church youth group meeting where I had spoken after the translation experience. Apparently I had explained to their astonishment how I had arrived and then proceeded to share my prepared message. After that I completely forgot about the incident until she reminded me that day.

Why was this? Why did I forget it? Well I think I know. This memory failure was of His doing. It was a miracle itself of the grace and mercy of God. He knew that at that time I would not have been able to tell others about it without basking in some of the glory myself. I've really had to examine my heart and motives whilst even sharing it now but I have had His permission to include it. This is so that 1) you will believe that you can expect to experience, as Jesus promised, those things that are described by Him as the "even greater than these things" and 2) that God's love and care for us is so great that He will go to any length to protect us and guard us from error.

Chapter 11: The Secret Chamber and Seeking His Face

"My heart says of you, "Seek his face!". Your face, Oh Lord, I will seek." Psalm 27:8

Some people call it their 'Trysting Place'. Others 'The Inner Chamber.' No matter what you call it, every child of God needs one. It is there that the clamour of life is exchanged for His Shalom (peace). It is there that you can know His Rest. It is there that the worries, anxieties and pre-occupations of life can be left behind outside the door. And it's there that God reveals Himself and His heart and enables you to know His Ways. It's there where He reveals your heart and heals its hurts and soothes its wounds. It is there that you begin to know His secrets and where He shares His dreams, purposes and plans. It's the place of fresh revelation and where God, who is the God of mysteries, becomes the God who is the Revealer of mysteries.

As I entered my Secret Chamber that first morning there was a real sense of God's presence. I was overwhelmed by His genuine willingness to communicate personally with me. I mean who was I, a mere creature, to commune with God the creator? He was and is the God of the Universe, as Jesus Himself would often say in prayer at the beginning of the Sabbath meal which begins..."Oh Lord God, King of the Universe".

The house where we were then living in was one Tricia and I had project managed at first and then eventually completed the building ourselves. We slept downstairs and lived upstairs because the house was perched on the side of a hill that overlooked the town below of Penryn in Cornwall, England. We enjoyed views of the old Brunel railway viaduct which linked the railway line between Truro and the coastal town of Falmouth and its beaches.

We could see the sea in the distance from our upstairs dining room windows. This room became my prayer chamber and I could sit at the dark mahogany table in this lovely dining room with its soft apple green walls, looking out of one of the two patio glass doors over the balcony. It was idyllic and so conducive to worship and prayer.

I sat on the high-backed carver chair and closed my eyes and began to reach out in my spirit to my Heavenly Father. Worship and praise began to flow out of my heart and the time seemed to just disappear. All this felt so right and the Lord was so well deserving of my worship but after a long while I remembered that I was supposed to be seeking the face of God as well and that must somehow mean looking into His eyes and letting him expose all He saw in me but that I couldn't see. Then it was also about asking Him to tell me what to do about what was being shown me and how to apply the blood of Jesus for cleansing and His Spirit for healing, restoration and transformation.

But if it was His face I was learning to gaze into then I would also see His lips and hear His voice. What would He say? Would He be angry or cross with me? Gentle or judgemental? But I needn't have worried because when He eventually broke into my consciousness

He laughed and said, "Where's your book?"

"What book?" I replied.

"The book you are going to write down all that I'm going to share with you as we meet each morning. I AM going to speak to you aren't I?"

And so began our conversations together.

"This is Tabernacle," He said one morning.

"Tabernacle?" I questioned. "What's that?"

I grabbed my Bible vaguely remembering something about Moses and the tabernacle and searched in Exodus. There it was written, 'The Tabernacle', and its meaning...the Tent of Meeting.

Exodus 33:7 "Now Moses used to take a tent and pitch it outside the camp, some distance away, calling it the 'tent of meeting."

"Are You going to meet with me like You did with Moses? Wow!"

Another morning the Holy Spirit asked me whether I knew that there was a protocol when approaching the Father in heaven. I said I didn't but I wanted to learn about it. He then went on to explain how so many of Father's children burst into His presence without an invitation or any introduction. "Of course they are always welcome," He said, "but I do wish that they would show just a little more respect. They come into God's presence hot and bothered and in a rush and sit on a chair sometimes as if back to front with a baseball cap on their head the wrong way around and chewing gum. Then they wonder why they fail to see Him there or hear His voice saying that He loves them so."

Another time I wanted to know more about God's nature or character. What He was really like.

As I began to ask Him, He quickly give me the most obvious of answers but one simply not followed by so many. "Why don't you read about people who knew Me better than you do right now, like Moses or Elijah, Samuel or David? It's all in My Word. Make notes in your book and learn what they discovered from their relationship with Me."

Occasionally I'd climb the stairs from my bedroom downstairs and walk into my Trysting Place knowing that I needed to meet Him through worship and adoration on that particular morning. This was a learning experience about myself as much as it was about the Father or Jesus or the Holy Spirit.

So that morning I went into the large family sitting room through the glass panelled adjoining French doors and lay full length on the carpeted floor and worshipped in tongues. Some ten minutes later I woke up to realise I'd dropped off to sleep.

"Oh no, I'm so sorry Lord. How could I do that?"

I dived into a self- pity pool and began to spiral downward in guilt.

"Stop that!" He cried out. "Don't beat yourself up. This is a part of the learning curve. Come on. Pick yourself up. Dust yourself down. Let's start again."

Some time later, I began to feel that my school teaching career was about to come to an end. If there was something else He was wanting me to do other than teaching then I really needed a fresh anointing. I was still meeting Him daily and often I talked to Him about abiding in His presence and dwelling under His anointing. I often found myself wondering what anointing was and I decided I would ask Him directly.

"Lord, What is anointing?" I questioned. For some time He remained silent.

"Lord, so much is written about anointing. There are volumes of books written on anointing. But would You give me Your definition of anointing and would You make it so simple and so clear that I can share it wherever I go in ministry?"

Still I waited.

Then He said "Write this down!"

I sat poised with pencil in hand ready to write.

"Anointing, Howard, is having My power and My presence within you.

You must have both for they are like two wings of a bird. Both are needed for balance and direction. Without both you only go around in circles.

Then, with My power and My presence within you, You will,

Preach it, and I'll bring conviction.

Teach it, and I'll bring revelation.

Command it, and I'll do it.

That is anointing."

On another occasion I wanted to know how a believer could know for certain when God was speaking to them and perhaps telling them to do something or when it was their own mind speaking and even deceiving them. "How can we tell?" I asked. "If you are truly seeking to know my heart and trying to walk in My ways," the Lord said, "Then the first thought you will have will be My thought, because you have the mind of Christ in you. There is usually a process of three thoughts. The first thought is My thought. The second thought is when reason sets in and doubt and questioning ensues and there is confusion. This is your own thought.

Finally there is the third thought. This is the devil coming along with his accusation making you feel inadequate or unworthy, suggesting that you could never know My mind anyway and then he successfully locks that mindset in place. What should you do in a time like that?" He asked rhetorically.

"Simply go back to the first thought and recapture the clarity of the Spirit's words and the peace it brought you. Take all thoughts once again and make them captive to Christ and then silence the voice of the enemy. Above all else, trust your intuition." Oh God's wisdom is so pure and peaceful isn't it?

These times of 'seeking God's face' were so precious. Needless to say these times of prayer not only changed my understanding of God Himself but transformed me too. Their purpose was to bring me to the place where eventually He would be able to share 'where' my journey was going and to 'whom' it had been taking me.

Chapter 12: Called and Chosen for Mission

"Ask of me, and I will make the nations your inheritance, the ends of the earth your possession." Psalm 2:8

"If ever we have a son we will call him Howard and maybe he will go to Africa instead of us." That was the cry of my mother's heart when finding that because of the Second World War she and dad could not go as missionaries to Rhodesia in the 1940's. Many years later in 2002 her prayer was fulfilled as then, having left teaching altogether, I was free to accept a mission invitation. I was going to Uganda. I said goodbye to Tricia and flew off for Western Uganda for two weeks to join a group of young men and women on a Scripture Union Evangelistic Crusade in several Ugandan Secondary Schools.

I first went out to Africa as an evangelist. It was such a privilege to preach the gospel and see many youths come to Christ. At that time I had no real understanding of the call on my life and the particular mandate He was going to place upon me one day and on my friend Mike Pike but there was much to learn about Him and His divine eternal purpose before ever we were ready for that. If part of being an apostle is to be a 'sent one' then being sure that He had sent me to Uganda albeit for evangelism was fulfilling at least a part of that future mandate.

In those first few years after leaving school I visited Uganda twice and Malawi three times. The first occasion I went to

Malawi was in my last year at Penryn School when I went with Tricia to find the orphan girl called Fiskani that Penryn School had been sponsoring for several years. During that visit I met Archbishop Harry Kaintano and his wife Ann. He was overseer of the African International Church (AIC) and Ann was a senior teacher at the Secondary School within the SOS Orphanage where Fiskani was. They lived in a small house within the same compound and were dedicated believers. Harry had an amazing testimony and his story was featured in one of Billy Graham's Ministry Decision Magazines.

As a teenager in the AIC Church Harry became a 'server' or an assistant to the priest. The AIC is a rather traditional Church in Malawi, but in his twenties although he was now married to Ann he began to lead an immoral life of womanising and drunkenness. He would be away from his home for months and then years, only returning home to Ann to get her pregnant again and increase a growing family. Finally for ten years he simply disappeared but Ann having herself got saved in a Salvation Army meeting in Malawi began to intercede for his salvation and return. "I pull him back. I pull him back," she would pray. For several years she prayed in faith that way and then one day there was a knock at her front door and there stood Harry. He was so repentant and wanted to come back. He told her that he too had got saved and knew the 'new creation' experience.

Ann remained cautious but had faith in him since this was what she had been praying for so accepted him back but under strict conditions which gave him a chance to prove his word, and he did. I met him many years later on this occasion

118

of our visit and he was now the Archbishop of the AIC. When he was ordained as Archbishop the first thing he did was to forbid drunkenness amongst his pastors or bishops as they were called and to outlaw bigotry. Both were rife in the AIC at that time but Harry showed great wisdom. He ruled that if any Bishop had more than one wife they were to remain faithful and impartial to all wives, but if one died they were to remain with the existing wife or wives and not marry again.

In the following years Harry not only reformed the whole AIC Church but had himself become baptised in the Holy Spirit. He wanted the AIC Bishops to receive the Spirit too so he invited his Pentecostal pastor friends into every one of his churches to teach them about the Holy Spirit and the Baptism and to pray for them. Revival came to the AIC before many months passed. Before I returned to the UK after this first visit, Harry invited me to come back for a one month tour of all his parishes in Malawi. I agreed to return as soon as possible.

A year later I was back and enjoyed an amazing whirlwind tour of all parts of Malawi from Rhumpi in the far north to the Shire Valley on the Mozambique border in the far south. We saw thousands saved and filled with the Spirit and many people supernaturally and instantly healed. I can only give space to one testimony here but there are dozens I could share. Harry had planned to hold a huge festival of praise for several of his parishes, their choirs and church members. It was to be in central Malawi and in a large Presbyterian Church on our way to the far north.

Unfortunately, when we arrived, we were met by the Presbyterian minister apologising profusely for a terrible double booking he had made and saying that we couldn't use his church or compound because he had a festival of his own that same weekend. I said that was not a problem and we offered to pray for the success of his event. We did that there and then and he was blessed. I told him that God knew about our situation and would therefore have already made alternative arrangements.

So we left to return home to Ann for the night and commissioned the Bishops who were the advanced party to seek God and find the place He really wanted us to go for the following Sunday morning service. When we returned back early the next day the Bishops had arranged for an open air service in a clearing that was in the middle of three neighbouring tribal settlements. Each of the settlements was in close view of the others but had a history of violent jealousy and altercations towards the others. But today despite the past, the elders had agreed to accept our request to hold our service in the middle of their separate territories and to take part or watch from a distance.

I had planned that we would pray for the sick after the choirs had sung and I had preached that morning but I wanted all the bishops to share in that ministry to the sick with me so I had arranged to meet them early before the service began to give them some teaching about healing and about how we might proceed together. The service began and there was great expectation. The worship songs by the many choirs were great. There was a sense of much excitement and joy.

I had asked all the Bishops to join me at the front of the service area and to sit either side of me on a row of upright dining room chairs brought with us from our homes. In front of these chairs was a long line of small low tables covered in white linen tablecloths. The congregation and choirs sat under the trees flanked by the people's homes in the distance and the villagers and chiefs sat on their chairs on their various verandas and would hopefully be listening and watching. Later Archbishop Harry introduced me and I was just about to begin my message when the Holy Spirit arrested me.

"Where are the elders or chiefs of the three tribes?" He asked. "I want you to honour them."

"Where are the elders of these communities?" I asked Harry.

"They are sitting on their verandas," was the reply.

"Go and ask them to come here. I want to honour them and invite them to sit here with the Bishops at the front."

Slowly all three men previously at war with each other made their way to the three places hurriedly provided for them and they took their seats. When they had sat down I expressed my gratitude for their generosity in letting us come at such short notice into their territory for this service. Then I began my sermon after which I gave a short appeal for Salvation making sure everyone understood clearly and then invited anyone who wanted God's forgiveness and the salvation He offered through Christ to come forward and to kneel at the front facing the bishops as a sign of their repentance.

Inviting the three elders to sit at the front was to make sure I had their full attention but that was God's initiative and not mine and they certainly had listened because the first three persons to respond and to be kneeling down and receiving Jesus as Saviour were the three elders; one from each of the warring tribes. Relationships between these communities were completely transformed and peace and healing came to that area. Apparently there were 3000 people present that day and Harry told me afterwards that over 1500 people received Salvation. The atmosphere was electric and full of faith for miracles. People were invited to come forward for healing and to line up in front of the Bishops to receive prayer. The people just flocked out.

I had said that the process we would follow for healing would be that I would pray first for the first person with the first Bishop next to me while he watched, listened and joined me by laying his hands on the sick person along with mine. As He saw the healing taking place and with his faith charged he would then pray on his own for the next person in front of him. I would move along the line repeating the procedure until every Bishop had witnessed a miracle and were moving in faith themselves in the Spirit. My little bottle of oil was being passed along between the Bishops and it seemed never to run dry. As people saw what God was doing there was such joy and thanksgiving. It was more like a party than a service. Hallelujah!

Suddenly I sensed a disturbance in my spirit and looking up I saw the village mad woman tottering in what looked like a drunken swagger in and out of the crowd, chattering in demonic whispers, hisses and obscenities. Some people were laughing at her and showing no compassion or concern. The Lion of Judah roared in me and I shouted out, "Stop laughing! How dare you laugh at her. She is a potential child of God. Now sit down all of you. Raise your hands towards her and pray for her."

I turned towards the demented woman. Her clothes were filthy. She had matted hair and many missing teeth and her sun scorched face was streaked with sweat and dirt. From where I stood I raised my finger towards her and shouted, "I bind you now in Jesus name!"

The woman was immediately thrown to the ground with a thud and was paralysed. In no way was I going to allow any attention seeking demon to interfere with this demonstration of Jesus's presence and power at work in His Church.

I walked over to where she was lying and urged the people to be quiet. I knelt down on the ground beside her to whisper in her ear what the Lord gave me to say. What came out of my mouth took me by surprise because I was about to give this demon or demons permission to stay inside her.

"I know you are there." I whispered in the woman's ear as she lay unconscious. "And I have the power and authority in Christ Jesus to command you to leave but I'm going to offer you permission to stay if you wish."

I was surprised by what I said and paused for a moment.

"However, I'm going to bring the blood of Jesus against you and that will burn you. It's your choice. Stay and experience the power of the blood or go to the place preserved and prepared for you as the Lord commands you. You will submit to Him. Are you ready? After three. One. Two. three. I bring the blood of Jesus against you!"

"Psssssss, aaaah!" And out of her ear they fled.

After a few moments the young woman who had looked previously in her eighties now stood upright and looked her actual age of around twenty three or so years old. She was now completely healed and in her right mind. She accepted Jesus as her Saviour and became a new creation in Jesus Christ. I suggested that she return to her family home and share the good news about what Jesus had done and that she had a bath and change of clothing. Then I questioned in my heart whether she had any other clothes because she had been in this state for several years now, so I asked if there was anyone there in the congregation that had a spare blouse or wrap-around skirt that she could have.

At first no one moved, probably questioning the reality of what they were witnessing, and then two young women in the crowd from two of the choirs slowly came forward and each offered a beautiful piece of clothing, folded so carefully. This was a costly thing to do for them and the Holy Spirit reminded me of Mary who broke the most precious and costly jar of perfume and poured it out over Jesus' feet. I thanked these two young women and said to them that like Mary this act of love and sacrifice would be talked about and celebrated in heaven that day.

Suddenly an elderly man standing near to me turned yellow white. He keeled over and fell to the floor, dead. People rushed to him and tried to resuscitate him but he was gone. "Spirit of death, release this man immediately!" I shouted. I was NOT going to allow Satan to steal any of God's glory. Right then the man convulsed and was violently sick vomiting up vulgar green fluids and blood. Men rushed to get water to throw over him and clean him up and as he returned to consciousness the first thing he shouted as he stood to his feet was, "Hallelujah! Hallelujah!" Then turning to the crowds he urged, "You must get saved. You must get saved."

Wow, what a day! A demonstration of the power of God. A learning curve in healing for the twenty Bishops. Thousands of salvations. Many, many healings. A deliverance and a resurrection from the dead, and the reconciliation and a restoration between three warring tribes. Thank you Jesus.

Archbishop Harry of Malawi was not the only servant of God from Africa I had the privilege of ministering with in those early days. But not all missions were as smooth as each other. These missions were where I cut my teeth. They were training times as well as an opportunity to experience the power of God at work. They were times where I got to know His 'works' but also His ways, His character and His heart, and His expectations. These missions were not an end in themselves but part of the training for what was to come. I was learning to climb the foothills in preparation for the real ascent that lay ahead.

Pastor Samuel from Nairobi, Kenya was another wonderful Man of God who travelled with me on this part of my 'Journey towards the Bridegroom'. I met Samuel at a crusade in Nairobi when I went as part of a team from England. He was on the African planning committee for the crusade but Samuel had been looking out for a white man he had seen in a vision a few months earlier.

The Lord had said that there was a particular assignment that He was joining Samuel to this white man for. When I saw Samuel at a crusade committee meeting the Lord pointed him out and told me that he had something to share with me so I introduced myself to him and asked what it was that the Lord had said to him. It was then that Samuel told me his story. From then on we began to mission together in obedience to the Father's word.

I joined Samuel on many visits all over Kenya and travelled with him, myself driving the car, throughout Western Kenya, up into Uganda and across to its western border and into Rwanda and then back again to Nairobi. It was a memorable series of crusades and conferences as well as a memorable drive.

Samuel was a leader among men particularly among the Pastors in Soweto, Kayole, a slum area on the outskirts of Nairobi where he and his family had chosen to live. He had brought the Pastors there together in unity and love and service to this deprived community and they had really made a difference. But since Church Unity was now a passion that the Lord had impressed on my heart too we sensed that for this particular season our partnership was anointed of God and so we began to minister specifically on unity.

We travelled throughout these three nations for about two months and held conferences in numerous places. En- route back to Nairobi after the three nation mission, we stopped off and ministered in Samuel's own family region of Kisumu and it was so good to stay with his parents in their rural community. It was there that we experienced another miracle of resurrection.

The last morning before we left Kisumu to travel back to Nairobi for a unity conference at Samuel's own Church in Soweto, I had been playing with a little child and then said goodbye to her and set off for Kenya's capital city. The conference began in the afternoon and we had a good opening morning session. However I was about to start again after a short break when suddenly I heard the Spirit say, "Pray for a little girl who has just died." So sure was I that I had heard God speak that I stopped the conference and explained what the Lord had just told me. So we all turned onto our knees and earnestly interceded for whoever this little girl was.

After about twenty minutes of prayer we all felt in our spirits that the work had been done and so continued with the teaching session. I noted the time. It was 3.15 pm. Later that day after the conference was over Samuel got a phone message from Kisumu to say that they had had a challenging day and went on to explain how the little girl that I had been playing with earlier that day from the village had eaten something at lunch time and choked on some food and suffocated. They couldn't save her and she choked to death.

They had to bury the little girl quickly since it was the very hot season in Kenya. They dug a shallow grave and placed the child in it in a shroud. Suddenly as they were throwing earth over her body the child convulsed and coughed and returned back to life. I asked what time it was when this happened and they said around 3.15pm that afternoon. It was when we sensed that we could stop praying. Praise God, this was no doubt the little girl the Lord had told us to pray for. Hallelujah! I love it when God does it His way.

As Samuel and I ministered together we saw many people delivered from demons. But I was also often disturbed by much of what I had seen in the deliverance ministry in Africa. It was often abused, and so was the person being delivered. Deliverance is often so noisy and unrighteous and dishonouring in the way it is ministered in Africa. It seems to be more about noise and enthusiasm than about authority and compassion.

It's certainly not about sensitivity towards the person in need. I teach that only one person should be praying or commanding any demon at any one time whilst others remain, perhaps standing around in internal or quiet prayer until it's their turn to minister and this should be done in as private a place as possible and not in the public arena unless unavoidable. If it is in public then it must be done with the greatest sensitivity towards the possessed who pare themselves victims and not the object of the prayer or commands. Not only do I teach this but at all times I would try to demonstrate it whenever on a mission.

I remember being in Uganda some years after that, with Mike Pike, who is now co- director with me of Call2Come. We were teaching about the Bride at an open-air conference but I noticed that every time a teaching session would begin a certain woman would come out from amongst the audience and stand in silent worship hands raised to heaven. She wasn't loud or consciously trying to be disruptive but I was disturbed in my spirit and shared it with Mike. I asked the Lord what He wanted us to do if anything. We always need to seek His guidance and permission.

"She has a religious spirit at work within her and is sent to disturb the conference but do not do anything yet. I'll tell you when," the Lord said. It was a day later that I saw her again and she was repeating this behaviour. The third day the Lord said, "It's time now."

The next conference speaker was already in full flow and it was important that there would be no noise or disturbance so I got up from my place and with my eyes fixed on her, though actually upon the demon within her, I began to walk silently towards her. I was about twenty five metres away. As I walked with my eyes fixed upon her I was silencing and binding the evil spirit in my spirit, but not making a sound with my voice. I was commanding in the spirit realm silently.

When I got within ten feet of her I raised my hand and with my index finger indicated the direction that the demon must go but still didn't make a sound. When I finally got close to her I flicked my long finger fast in the direction towards the right and the spirit left her and she collapsed over my shoulders. The demon was gone.

"He is gone now." I said quietly. "It's ok. You can sit down in your seat again. He won't come back."

She was free and very few people noticed anything. Remember, noise and enthusiasm is no substitute for authority! It is so important too that we never presume anything when partnering in ministry with the Lord. Learning to listen to His instructions and only doing what He says and when He says, is vital. We simply ask Him what we should do and then follow His instructions. It's when we go beyond His boundaries or brief, or disrespect His timing and His permission, that errors or confusion occur. These principles were so clearly illustrated when with Samuel we held a crusade in the centre of a small rural village in Kenya.

We had taken a group of pastors with us from the region to counsel those seeking salvation and to minister in prayer for healing or deliverance after the message had been preached. Many people responded to the gospel and many others came forward for prayer with the team of pastors standing at the front. I was standing amongst them.

A woman came to me carrying a very large young boy. I found out that he was a three year old and totally paralysed. His mother and father were distraught with worry and getting to the point where they were becoming unable to care for him because of his weight and inability to do anything for himself. He was so heavy and as she held him to herself he just hung limply over her shoulders and arms.

As was my usual practice I asked the mother what was wrong and then suggested that we ask the Father what was causing the child's paralysis. We didn't have to wait long for His answer. The Father explained so simply that it was a matter of connection and communication. The connection between the body, brain and the muscles via the nerves of this young boy's body had completely broken down. As a result there was no communication and therefore no muscle or limb response.

"You command the nerves of his body to activate and I'll make it happen," the Lord said. This we did, in Jesus name, and then I sent them all home and suggested that they put the boy to bed and allow the Holy Spirit and the angels to do what they do best, while he slept. At about 6 am the following morning there was a scream and a shout and the mother came running into the village centre and to where we were lodging crying out, "He's healed. He's healed. He's washing himself, sitting up in his bath, for the first time in his life. Oh Hallelujah!"

Chapter 13: Learning by Observation and Revelation

"I pray, that all of them may be one, Father, just as you are in me and I am in you. May they also be in us so that the world may believe that you have sent me." John 17:21.

"And God placed all things under his feet and appointed him to be head over everything for the church, which is his body, the fullness of him who fills everything in every way." Ephesians 1: 22-23.

These early missions were a real learning experience for me. Yes, I learnt much about how to minister His grace and healing power and about the authority of both His name Jesus or Yeshua, and His Blood and about what TO do and what NOT to do in matters like deliverance. But much of this learning was through observation and reflection as I took it all to him in that 'Secret Place'. I still kept that 'Place' even while on a mission. It was a time of intense observation and precious revelations.

One of the most painful observations I made throughout these trips around the nations was about His Church. I was devastated by the obvious fact that the Church of Jesus Christ was so broken and so divided. I knew it caused Him so much pain firstly because the Church is His body and he feels the pain of His own body and secondly because it was what He prayed most for, that the Church would be One.

In John 17:21 He prayed, "I pray that they will all be one, Father, just as you are in me and I am in you. May they also be in us so that the world may believe that you have sent me." Yet over 2000 years later, it's still in disorder, and more importantly in division.

It's true that familiarity breeds contempt and that my own familiarity with the variety of different churches that there are in England didn't help me to see that the same lack of Church unity existed here in the UK as in other nations. It is just that the cultural and environmental differences experienced in another country often cause these things to be seen more clearly.

During my missions to Africa over the next few years I ministered in about ten different nations and yet I found a divided church that knew little about what unity was. I saw in every city a multiplicity of churches whose congregations met in small metal corrugated buildings found on every corner or along the main street in the community. In Nigeria for example I counted 20 different churches along a short stretch of the same street and from enquiries made with various pastors, I found that very few of these churches had anything to do with each other.

It was the same story in the main towns or capital cities of Uganda, Kenya, Malawi, Ghana and many more. Each tin hut would display a huge sign announcing the name of the church. A pair of loud speakers would be arranged at each corner to project the amplified sounds of the worship inside and the sermon and especially the prayers in tongues, towards the bemused or confused unbelievers who lived around in the community. It was an invasion of others' privacy and space. This I found so offensive and insensitive and was, it seemed to me, such an ineffective witness. I was so disturbed by what I saw and decided to commit myself to preach and to teach about the Father's heart for unity of His Son's Church and to help to see the fulfilment of Jesus' prayer in John 17:21. This soon became the central theme of any conference I held.

Some time later during this season I was invited to speak at an International Conference on Church Unity in Benin, West Africa. It was held in the huge national auditorium built by the Chinese. The Presidents of Benin opened the conference. When I was invited to the platform to speak they introduced me as Pastor Howard Barnes from the UK, the Apostle of Unity. Everything within me rebelled against that title and at first I rejected it basically because I just hated titles. But then I thought "No. I'll take that. I'll accept that." I knew that this longing for unity in the Church was the deepest desire of Jesus' heart and I was willing to carry that mantle with honour.

So for this next few years I spent most of my time travelling around the nations preaching and holding conferences about the Body of Christ and Jesus' desire for Unity. I would expose the divisiveness and jealousy within the Church between pastors and plead for repentance and a brokenness of spirit and a humility of heart that should be the very character of any pastor.

God anointed us this season and we saw much reconciliation and healing between churches in the cities where we ministered. I would share about the things I'd observed on my journeys and teach the principles they illustrated and point out the scriptural foundation for these truths. One day at a conference, I wanted to explain how the brokenness of the Body causes Jesus such pain and I shared the experience that I had had in Malawi when I cut my foot. God used these experiences to show me so many truths and He wanted me to share them.

I was in a village in Malawi and they had provided me with a wonderful round village house to sleep in. The house had a small door and several small shuttered windows spaced out around the circular walls of the house. The owners had taken out all their furniture but left there a single bed and a small low bedside table and a chair. The bed was a metal framed spring bed with heavy solid legs at each corner and across the springs they had laid planks of wood with a blanket spread over them. On the bedside table was a candle and some matches, some fruit and a bottle of water. I sat down on the bed testing the gentle bouncing movement of the springs designed to rock me to sleep. I retired quite early that night as I was tired and when all the window shutters were closed it was very dark.

Now being a man of mature years, like many I needed to relieve myself during the night and so woke up in a room in absolute pitch black darkness. I needed to find the small door to get outside and so put my hand out towards where I believed the candle and matches were in order to light it and knocked it off the table. I heard it sliding across the floor. It was then that I remembered I had a torch in my case and so fumbled for it in the dark. I switched it on with great anticipation only to discover that its battery was flat. "Oh no," I sighed.

Nervously I began to make my way towards where I thought the door was but couldn't find it and so thinking I was perhaps disoriented I turned around and walked across the room to where I hoped the door was the other side. But no, I walked straight into one of the heavy legs of the metal bed splitting my little toe nail. It hurt badly and I sensed it was bleeding.

I sat down in the dark on the bed nursing my injury.

"Does it hurt?" Jesus asked.

"Of course, a lot," I cried and continued to hold my toe in the dark.

There was a long silence. All thoughts of going outside were now gone.

Then Jesus said, "Where else do you feel the pain?"

I thought for a moment and then answered, "In my stomach. It makes me feel sick in my stomach".

"Yes. That is like my body too. When one part hurts the other parts hurt too. When the Baptist Church is hurting the Pentecostal Church hurts as well."

This sudden realisation deeply affected me and made me even more passionate to see unity in the Body of Christ.

Finally after another pause the Lord asked me one more question.

"Howard, where did you register and first become conscious of that pain?

"In my head," I replied after some thought.

"Yes, and I am the head of My Church and I feel its pain".

Why was it, I thought, that so many in the Church do not see this? Why are they so wrapped up in just 'doing church,' in programmes and in performance, but not aware of what it means to be The Church and how it affects Jesus who is our Head? Do they not think about His thoughts and His feelings? Do they not sense His pain?

The following day I was to receive a revelation which gave me some answers to these questions. Jesus showed me clearly the true state of His Church and why it was so insensitive to His heart. The reason was because it had become disconnected to Him who was its head. The revelation I received concerned a chicken.

It was getting close to dinner time and the ladies were busy preparing. I was chatting with them. Suddenly a chicken came around the corner pecking at the ground. I watched him for a moment not knowing that this was about to become my dinner. A little later I heard a screech and a thud coming from that area of the kitchen and wondered what it was, but then a headless chicken came charging around the corner of one of the houses. It was our dinner, the chicken had made the ultimate sacrifice.

But as I watched, this headless chicken began to run around in ever decreasing circles flapping its wings furiously and then keeled over and fell down, lifeless. Then the Lord spoke into my spirit again so strongly. "This is like my Church. She's become so disconnected to her Head and I am the Head of the Church. She is busy making such a lot of noise and flapping her wings with much activity but is just going around in circles. She's busy going nowhere because she's lost connection with me, her head."

We lose connection with our Head when as a Church we begin to lose connection with each other. When we disrespect and abuse the Body by pursuing an independent and worse still a competitive course, we eventually lose the favour and anointing of God and become disconnected. Conversely, Psalm 133 reminds us, "where brothers dwell together in unity, there the Lord (the Head) bestows the blessing." It's here that our witness is the strongest for as He said, He desires this unity "so that the world may believe."

I have been privileged to experience the power of this witness several times after a conference with people running up to us to congratulate us, somehow sensing a change in the spiritual atmosphere. Many times at the end of a Conference we would have a united march of witness through the streets by the pastors and even muslims would run up to us saying, "You've exorcised the demons in this area by that demonstration of unity."

There were two very special occasions, both in Africa, when we witnessed such a move of reconciliation and unity between the churches. One was in Bushenyi in Uganda, the other in Bungoma in Western Region, Kenya.

I had received an invitation by Apostle Peter Kamanzi from Bushenyi, a large town in the western area of Uganda near to the Rwandan border, to hold a Conference on unity. Peter had worked so hard to break down the walls of division between the churches in Bushenyi. There was a feeling of great expectation that I could feel as soon as I arrived and the conference flowed so well and a heavy sense of conviction of unrighteousness and the need to repent fell upon all participants.

I called for prayer and asked each pastor to turn to find another pastor and confess any bitterness or resentment or unforgiveness that was being revealed by the Holy Spirit that was in their heart. What I witnessed was a sovereign act of God. There were many tears and yet great joy all mixed together. I saw two pastors after praying for each other climb on the back of the other as the spirit fell upon them and they spun round and around in the spirit with much laughter and joy. Love and grace flowed. Honour and respect for each other abounded.

Soon after this time of celebration had ended, a group of pastors came to me with a request. They wanted large sheets of paper and some felt- tip pens because they wanted to make large placards with this sentence blazoned across it. "We are the Pastors of Bushenyi. There is now only one Church in Bushenyi." What a statement! Then they said they wanted to go on a march of witnesses through the main street of Bushenyi proclaiming this truth.

So we marched to the four corners of the town demonstrating this unity and at each corner hammered in a stake with scriptures written on them taking possession of the territory for Jesus. A powerful victory was gained that day and there was an open heaven.

On the way to the last corner we passed the witch-doctor's house. I knew this only because the pastor marching besides me told me so with the added comment, "Oh he's so powerful. He rules this area."

The Lion of Judah roared again in me deep down in my soul. "How dare you proclaim that!" I exclaimed. "'You have just committed high treason. You have taken the things of the King and given them over to another." It was both a revelation and a rebuke and we both learnt a lot from that experience.

As we passed the witch- doctor's house I left the march and climbed up the dark red Ugandan soil and grassy bank into the witch-doctor's garden. A man came around the side of the house towards me and I could see by the things he was wearing of bone and shells that it was him. He bore down on me like an angry bull but the love of Christ consumed me and gave me such peace.

"Hello," I said. "I'm Pastor Barnes from England. Can I give you a hug in Jesus name?"

And we hugged each other, though complete strangers, for what seemed like five minutes. I heard deep within my spirit the words, "The love of God is shed abroad in your hearts by faith." Then I said to him, "I just wanted to tell you that God our heavenly Father doesn't want you to do these things any more (referring to his witchcraft). They are only hurting you and others around you. He wants you to know Him and receive His blessings but to receive that, you need to repent and turn your heart over to Him. I have come from England to tell you that."

There and then conviction came upon him and he turned to Christ and got saved. That was soon followed by the salvation of his whole family a few days later. I said goodbye and re-joined the march.

Our walk back to the church from the last corner was continuously interrupted by people running out of their houses to beg us to enter and to pray for them. Truly the Spirit of God was moving and heaven had come down.

I was almost dragged into one home and asked what was going on. I explained and shared the gospel and immediately they all responded and accepted salvation. Then I noticed an old lady lying on the floor in this single roomed dwelling. I asked what was wrong with her and they told me that she had been paralysed for many years and so she just lay there. I declared that she would get up and dance with me in Jesus' name and commanded her to be healed. She immediately leapt to her feet and we danced all around that room together much to the surprise and great joy of all present.

Years later I was back in Bushenyi for another conference and ministry with Apostle Peter and I knew that there was some unfinished work to do at the witch-doctor's house. I shared this with Peter and even though I knew that since his salvation the witchdoctor had died, I needed to return to the house in the centre of Bushenyi.

Peter and I took the short walk in that direction wondering what unfinished business was still to be done. As we reached the garden, I saw a young woman weeding around the vegetables growing there. She was the daughter of the witchdoctor and Peter pointed her out to me telling me that she was totally deaf and dumb. I knew then what the Lord wanted to complete. Her disabilities were a direct result of her father's demonic activities because the devil is no one's friend and he always brings suffering and destruction to everyone he entraps, either to them personally or those they love.

I asked Peter to introduce me to her and then I asked her if I could pray for her and break the hold on her life caused by the father's satanic involvement so she could be healed. She accepted and with great expectation we prayed together and took authority over the works of the devil. Suddenly she began to say, "Jesus! Jesus! Hallelujah!" She had begun to speak. Oh thank you Lord Jesus. She could now speak and hear.

That march of witness we had held in Bushenyi was wonderful and brought many to Christ but perhaps the march held in Soweto, Kayole slums, outside Nairobi, Kenya, with Apostle Samuel, was the one that physically changed the landscape of that area in the most practical way possible. It was here in this poor slum that we marched in unity, prayed, decreed and declared a physical change in the environment wherever we stopped. We prophesied that a new sewage system, tarmaced roads and electricity would come to this deprived area within a year. Within twelve months of returning home to England Samuel told me that these things had been completed by the local council.

And just in case you think that these are isolated incidents and unusual miracles, let me record just one more. This is what happened in Bungoma, Western Region Kenya, in 2008 after a similar conference on unity there.

We arranged, after the conference, at the request of the participating Pastors, another March of Witness, this time through the streets of Bungoma, but there were many, many more pastors involved on this occasion. Much work towards unity had gone on for years in Bungoma through the ministry of a local leader, Pastor Martin Sikuku. I would go to Bungoma for two or three weeks at a time to minister with him. Then later I met Rev. David Munby in England, now a close friend of ours, who was an English Anglican priest but also serving as the Canon of Bungoma. David would take time out from his parish church in Barnsley, England to go to Bungoma and serve the Anglican Church there. He was a worshipper and an intercessor and his church in Barnsley was known as a House of Prayer for all Nations.

I first met David at a conference in London where I was speaking, and discovering our mutual interest in Bungoma and our desire to see the Church there united, we started travelling together there on mission (later we also missioned together in India). (Interestingly, Mike Pike had also developed a close friendship with Pastor Martin Sikuku, and often shared in ministry with him.)

David has a lovely wife called Jill and later on Mike and I had the privilege of going to India again as a team with Jill Munby and the Rev. Patricia Torok from the USA, to share the message of the Bride. It was a precious time since it was one of the first missions in which Mike and I had felt confident and clear enough to share what the Lord was showing us about His heart concerning the Bride. It was one of the first Bridal conference ministry trips.

But now, back to Bungoma. So here we were, all three of us, serving the Lord together from different Church backgrounds and experiences, an African Pentecostal Pastor called Martin, an Anglican Priest from the UK called David, and myself, an ex-Salvationist, a confirmed Anglican, and now a 'one Church' missionary with a Pentecostal experience.

The conference was so blessed and once again we arranged a march of witness of unity to conclude the event. About five hundred pastors this time took part in the march through this busy and very large town but one thing was a disappointment to us: the Bishops or denominational leaders of the various churches in Bungoma had not attended the conference and consequently were not in the march. But God had his master-plan.

I had managed through my Salvation Army connection to get the Bungoma Salvation Army band to lead the march and we set off on what was a long route around the area. The police were in attendance too. What we didn't realise however was that our route would take us past the very large Roman Catholic Church which was holding a Confirmation service and First Communion for a very large number of children and young people. All their parents and relatives were attending of course and as we approached the building where the service had just finished, they all poured out dressed in their best and the communicants in their white dresses or pure white trousers, shirts and shoes. They looked magnificent.

"What's the march about?" they asked.

"Oh, it's a march of witness for Jesus and to show our love for Him." I said.

"Can we join you?" they asked.

And so our march swelled in number by almost one hundred as parents joined in too.

But the final blessing, all pre- arranged by the Lord but entirely unknown to us, was that further along this main town road was the hotel where the very Bishops who had chosen not to attend our conference were meeting.

They heard the Salvation Army Band, came out onto the hotel balcony and read the placards, realised who we were and were convicted and 'provoked to jealousy'. Some time later I got a communication from them apologising for not supporting the Unity Conference and asking me to arrange another conference in Bungoma as soon as possible because they wanted to attend.

These experiences were key markers in my 'Journey of Ascent', but I realised as I reflected on them after returning to England again that Jesus' prayer in John 17 was not that we should be united but that we should be 'One'. Yes He would bless unity as He promised in Psalm 133, but He desired more than that. In Psalm 133 God declares that we are to 'dwell' together in unity.

It was not to be a five minute wonder but a state of mind and heart; a dwelling together. That sort of unity was not dependent on the length of a united project or a three day conference, a unity that lasted only as long as the event. With these principles firmly established in my spirit I was getting ready for the revelation that would change my life forever. The Church's True Identity. In fact He wasn't actually asking us for unity at all. He was asking for a deeper transformation of our very corporate being as believers, which was a product of a 'Oneness' that flowed out from a relationship of 'Oneness' experienced with Him.

I sensed it was more about intimacy with Him first and from this intimacy would come a revelation of who we really were in Christ. It was not just that we were sons and daughters of the Father but it was about who we were to Jesus, His Son. And not just as individuals but corporately together.

I had been to boot camp and now I'd scaled the foothills. I was about to begin my ascent to the mountain tops. The real journey was about to begin. It was upwards and onwards and was a journey towards the Bridegroom. What I didn't know yet was that this journey would not be taken alone. I was soon to meet someone who would be a fellow traveller and fellow climber.

Part 2: The Journey Upwards and Onwards

Chapter 14: A Meeting at the Well

"And Rebekah went down to the spring (well), filled her jar and came up again." Genesis 24:16.

It was January 2008, and 'my' journey was soon to become 'our' journey for it was at a well that I met Mike.

I had arranged to attend the first meeting of the year of the CPI, that is, the Cornwall Prayer Initiative. This is an association of individuals and small prayer groups who meet regularly to intercede for the advance of God's kingdom in our county, or region, of Cornwall, England. Although the prayer meetings throughout the year were by individual arrangement the first meeting of the year was a gathering of all intercessors for prayer and planning. This gathering was precious and was like meeting at a well of 'living water'.

A new visitor to Cornwall called Mike Pike was introduced to us all at this meeting. He had come to live in the county with his family because the Lord had led him to do so. Jo, Mike's wife, worked for the National Health Service. Mike shared a little about his journey of intimacy with the Lord and it resonated deeply with me. His experience had been so similar to mine.

We decided to meet up for further fellowship but somehow it didn't happen and it wasn't till twelve months later at the next annual CPI meeting that we met again and this time we arranged to have coffee together in a small café in Liskeard, Cornwall, near where Mike lived. The Holy Spirit moved so strongly upon us as we talked together over that drink and we both sensed that God was at work doing something quite extraordinary.

That night as I was reflecting on the meeting, the Spirit reminded me of the story in Genesis 24 of Eliezer finding a wife for Isaac. The fact that Abraham was looking for a bride for his son and Eliezer found her at the well somehow connected to both Mike's and my experience. It was as if it was an illustration of something so much more profound that the Lord was about to reveal to both of us. The well from where Rebekah drew the water was symbolic of the well of life from which we both were learning to draw. Both of us had discovered our own Secret Well where we met the Lord each day, in the place of intimacy.

At the well Rebekah met Eliezer who wanted to take her on a journey to find her bridegroom and we both knew somehow that that was the direction He was leading us in too, toward our Bridegroom King. The meeting of each other at the CPI gathering was destined to change our lives in a most wonderful way.

In 2009 Mike and his son Ben and I shared another mission assignment to Kenya, firstly to Nairobi and then up to Bungoma in Western Region, and soon after that Mike and I were travelling everywhere together. This would begin a friendship and a partnership in ministry that would last for many years to come. Our assignment in Bungoma was to hold a conference for the Bishops. It was the consequence of my visit to Bungoma the previous year when we held that March of Witness that 'provoked the Bishops to jealousy' and caused them to invite us back for a conference which they would now attend.

This visit was one year after the terrible consequences of the National Elections in Kenya where relationships between communities had broken down and things had escalated into terrible ethnic violence. In addition to the Bishop's Conference we also held a conference on reconciliation and unity in the Mt Elgon area where such atrocities and ethnic hatred had caused great division amongst even the Pastors, setting those from the north against those from the south.

The conference was well received but we were aware that the pastors from the northern area were sitting together in one section and the pastors from the southern area in another. There wasn't a bad atmosphere amongst the participants but there still wasn't any real demonstration of reconciliation. After both Mike and I had shared the message that God had laid upon our hearts we had planned to ask the pastors from both the north and the south to step forward and to stand in a line opposite each other at the front and then to encourage them to ask each other for forgiveness and to pray for one another.

However suddenly we saw that we couldn't do this until we as British Colonial 'whites' had knelt down and humbled ourselves before them and asked forgiveness from them for the way we, as the British nation, had mistreated our Kenyan brothers in the days leading up to their National Independence years and years previously. The British had dealt with the resistance to British rule under the British Empire so harshly and held such freedom fighters known as the Mau Mau in what were best described as concentration camps reminiscent of Nazi Germany.

So Mike and I made our confession and asked them for their forgiveness and graciously these pastors from both sides flooded out to the front to embrace us. Then they turned to each other and with tears of genuine repentance hugged each other and forgive one another too. Reconciliation was now made and healing received. Hallelujah!

Mike and I both had our separate ministry names at that time. I was ministering under the banner of 'The Body and the Bride' and Mike under 'Time Out Mission'. Time Out Mission was about 'taking time out' on a number of levels. It spoke about the need to make that personal space in the business of one's life by taking 'time out'. It was also about seeking God and developing intimacy with Him. It also emphasised the reality of Jesus' return in this End-Time; that time was running out and of our need to be prepared for Jesus' return.

The Body and the Bride on the other hand was about unity of the Body and the oneness of all believers as in John 17 so that from that starting point the Church might come to understand the bridal nature of that oneness and seek to prepare herself as His precious Bride ready for His return. But at that time my own bridal consciousness was just awakening and I had caught so far only a glimpse of what we now refer to as the 'Bridal Paradigm'.

Around that time I had accepted an invitation to speak in the main meeting of the National Church Unity Conference in Benin, West Africa and also to take a workshop. Mike joined me again and he and I shared the workshop together. We had begun to appreciate more and more the spiritual battles that rage in the heavenlies when you preach about unity. Later on we were to experience even fiercer enemy opposition as we began to teach about the Bride and so began to appreciate how precious the Bride must be to the Lord.

The night after the conference in Benin, Mike and I were woken-up by a loud clap of thunder to witness an incredible storm raging in the skies all above the city. Lightning bolts flashed repeatedly followed immediately by horrendous clashes of thunder that reverberated in the very earth itself beneath our feet. It felt that the hotel was rocking under this assault of the demonic, manifesting in nature. I asked the Lord what was going on and He said that these were the maritime and marine spirits thrashing around in anger at the proclamation of the Truth and the message of Unity.

From Benin we flew to Liberia and met Dr Kortu Brown, one of the key Church leaders in that nation who is now President of the Liberian Council of Churches (LCC). I had ministered for him before, a few years earlier, but now we began to build what would be an ongoing close relationship with this nation and members of the Christian leadership there.

Ministering together with Mike but under separate ministry titles seemed now incongruous since we were wanting to demonstrate our own unity. But we began to sense that the Lord was not bringing our ministries together for partnership but for a merger. After much prayer I laid The Body and The Bride name down and for a time we both ministered as Time

Out Mission. However God had His own plans and soon a new ministry was to be born with a new name and one that would reflect our calling and mandate.

Meanwhile there was still much yet for the Lord to show us. There were fresh understandings and revelations about the Bride and the Bridegroom that we needed to receive before we were ready for that new development. We had only just begun to take this exciting climb together. But new revelations were being given and shared together and this accelerated our learning experience. We continued to 'seek His face' and meet Him individually in our 'Trysting Places' and to mission and conference together around the nations sharing all that which He had shown us thus far about our bridal identity.

Our mandate was now becoming clearer, our calling more understood. It was a blessed call and an awesome call. It was less about the Body now and more about the Bride. It was to awaken and prepare the Bride for the Wedding of the Lamb and for Jesus to return again. It was to get a generation of His Body ready for that day of the wedding.

One of my favourite Christian songs of all time had been 'I want to fulfil the purposes of God in my generation'. This End-time generation would welcome the Lord and be anointed with the 'Spirit of Elijah'. It would be so dedicated to Jesus and it would carry a John the Baptist mandate to 'Prepare the way of the Lord', to announce that Jesus was coming back and to align itself with the Spirit and cry "Maranatha, Come Lord Jesus."

As the importance of this cry for Jesus to come started to take root in our hearts the recognition of a new ministry name began to form in our minds. This would result in the formation of the ministry which we oversee today- Call2Come International Ministry, but we intuitively understood that it was not to be so much a ministry as part of a 'movement of God', the Bridal Movement, that would prepare the way for His coming again.

Chapter 15: The Wake-Up Call

"Come, I will show you the bride, the wife of the Lamb." Revelation 21:9

"My lover said to me, 'Arise, my darling, my beautiful one, and come with me." Song of Songs 2:10

It was a great joy to travel on a mission with Mike and this enabled us to spend much more time together especially during the long air flights, sharing the new revelations about the bride we were both receiving. But how you might ask, did I myself first come to understand the message of the Bride and the mandate we were now to carry together? Well, I was in the presence of the Lord one morning reflecting with the Lord on the wonderful things He had done during the previous missions I had been on. Suddenly He spoke so clearly but so sadly and it saddened me too.

"Hmm, yes Howard. It was a good time and indeed many became members of my heavenly family. But oh, the earthly expression of that family, My Son's Church there on earth, She is having a real crisis."

"What do you mean Father?" I cried out.

"She is having a crisis of identity. Not only is she so divided but, She doesn't know who she is," He said. My immediate response was one of shock.

"She? She?" I hesitated,, " Is the Church...a, a woman?" I questioned.

"Yes," He replied, "though not in a gender sense. She is the most beautiful woman I've ever created and she's formed from all my adopted children; from every born again believer; Jew and Gentile and from every tribe, colour and race upon this earth, from times past, present and future. They are mine but from them I've created the most beautiful being, the most beautiful of all my creation, a Bride, and I'm giving her as a love gift to My Son."

This revelation reminded me of a vision I had experienced some months earlier when praying about another mission I was about to go on, whether it was to Africa or India or Colombia in South America, I cannot remember now. I was seeking Him for a fresh anointing for this assignment and became conscious that I also needed a deeper inner cleansing and sanctification. My mind was full of all the many spiritual gifts that I needed from Him to fulfil the mission, all which were equally important. It was as if I was looking at the facets of a most beautiful diamond. The diamond itself was a very precious stone and glistened and sparkled brilliantly. I could see it quite clearly. It was magnificent. These gifts which I desired were but facets of this diamond.

"Lord Jesus, I know that these things I'm asking you for are so important but I sense they are just facets of something else. I can see a diamond in my spirit. Yes, truly it is glorious, so pure and so perfectly formed. Please, please tell me. What is the diamond?" For quite some time He was silent. Then He said, "It's my Bride. These are just glimpses of her beauty."

This revelation ignited a deep longing within me to know more about the Bride. "Oh tell me more," I pleaded. "Read Psalm 45," was His answer. I hurriedly turned to it and found that underneath the title Psalm 45 in my Bible were the words, 'The Psalm about the Bride'. Oh I was so moved. I didn't know this. I was so blessed as I read the text describing the majesty of the Bridegroom and the sheer beauty of the Bride.

"Oh tell me more. Please tell me more!" I begged. Read Revelation 21:9, "Come I will show you the bride, the wife of the Lamb." Although I knew that this was a message and vision given to John the Apostle, I felt the Spirit was talking directly to me and it was also a promise to me. Little did I know at that time that Mike too was receiving similar revelations. This experience about the Bride was set to change the focus of our ministry forever.

However we were also aware that the revelation that we are His Bride and are being prepared for Jesus and for the Wedding of the Lamb is a concept which is too much for many to embrace. That they are children of the Father and that Jesus is their Saviour is wonderful but the thought of being a bride and of being 'given away' to another by the Father is too much. But God is so gracious so the Spirit of God seeks first to develop our relationship with the Father as His sons and daughters so that we will become mature and secure in His love.

This teaching about God's love as our Father is deeply rooted in scripture but in very recent times the Holy Spirit has brought to His people a fresh emphasis and significance to it. It has been popularised by the 'Father Heart of God' Movement. So there are two revelations that we need to embrace. This first revelation is that we were chosen to be children of the Father by a glorious spiritual adoption.

The second is that we are chosen to be the bride of Christ, Father's Son and this revelation is one that is reserved for the end times. Both revelations are to do with our identity.

Let's look first in more detail at the first revelation which is about our relationship to the Father as His sons and daughters.

It was so necessary that this revelation came first before the revelation about our Bridal identity because as we will see this revelation produces the necessary maturity and security within the believer as they experience the Father's love. No Father on earth will give away his daughter to be a child bride. Both mother and father will teach and train her in all manner of home skills and seek to imbibe wisdom and develop character in their beloved until one day she's ready for marriage, mature and prepared. Would not the Father of all fathers want such a bride to be given to His own Son? So first we belong to the Father as His children.

In fact it was always the Fathers plan that He would have spiritually born children. It was ever His eternal purpose that we should be His adopted children and grow in His love towards that maturity. Ephesians 1:4-5 tells us this. "In love he predestined us to be adopted as his sons through Jesus Christ, in accordance with his pleasure and will." This was why we were saved and redeemed.

Galatians 4:5-7 says that the Father chose "to redeem those under law, that we might receive the full rights of sons. Because you are sons, God sent the Spirit of his Son into our hearts, the Spirit who calls out, "Abba, Father." And this is something that begins the moment we receive salvation through the cross, for scripture says in John 1:12 "Yet to all who received him, to those who believed in his name, he gave the right to become children of God."

But it doesn't stop there; 1 John 3:2 tells us, "Dear friends, now we are children of God, and what we will be has not yet been made known. But we know that when (Jesus) appears, we shall be like him, for we shall see him as he is."

Oh how precious is this? Fully like Him in His very nature, and so becoming completely compatible with Him, able to be joined to Him as His Bride.

As I studied further the early chapters of Genesis I was reminded of the teaching of Paul in Romans 5 v 14 where Adam was described as a pattern of the one to come (Jesus) and of 1Corinthians 15 v 45 about Jesus being the Last Adam.

In Genesis 2:23 it says that it was "not good for the first Adam to remain alone" so God created for him a partner, a Bride. Was it not also in the purposes of God that His own Son should not 'remain alone'. Father had planned to give Him a bride would be a corporate being made up of everyone who believed in Him and yet to enable this to be so, He, like a grain of wheat would need to die to self and be buried in order to produce many more seeds. As it says in John 12:24 "unless a kernel of wheat falls to the ground and dies, it

159

remains only a single seed. But if it dies it produces many seeds." These many seeds are His 'offspring' that He travailed for as it says in Isaiah 53=.

"Yet it was the Lord's will to crush him and cause him to suffer and though the Lord makes his life an offering for sin, he will see his offspring..... and be satisfied". Isaiah 53 :10 and 11.

Through His death we become those who would make up His Bride. Isn't this wonderful?

And isn't it wonderful to be a child of the Father too? We join with John when he says in 1 John 3:1, "How great is the love the Father has lavished on us, that we should be called children of God! And that is what we are!"

But what does it actually mean to be adopted? Two things happen in our relationship to God's family the moment we believe in Christ as our Saviour. The believing sinner, who is not a natural son or daughter of God, is repositioned as an adult son in the family of God. And this is a legal action and position. It is like a formal adoption or the legal 'placing' of a child in a new family. It is an act of God which places the believer in His family as an adult son or daughter.

At the same time we are told in the Scriptures that the believer is not only placed legally but spiritually born again of His nature into the family of God. This is the new birth or regeneration and so in a sense we are as a child who then needs to grow and develop.

So 1) we are legally placed into His family as an adult son and daughter and inheritor of all Father has, and 2) we are born again and therefore a babe in Christ who needs to grow up to become like Him and mature. However the believing sinner's position, having been adopted as His son or daughter, is one of full privilege in the family of God even from the very moment of rebirth and adoption.

When the Apostle Paul speaks of our spiritual adoption by God he uses the Greek word huiosthesia (huios - a son) (thesis - a placing), which means 'to place as a son'. It is the place given to one to whom it does not belong, nor merits it, but it is theirs by faith.

Galatians 3:26 says, "You are all sons of God through faith in Christ Jesus." So adoption puts the emphasis on the position we have with God as His children because of God's grace in response to our faith. But it is our responsibility from then on to allow the Holy Spirit, who indwells every believer with His presence and power, to transform us and conform us to His likeness so that "Christ be formed in us".

Let's say it again. When a lost sinner enters into the very family of God, He does so undeservingly. God in His amazing love, grace and mercy has taken us – the lost, helpless, poverty-stricken, debt-laden sinner and adopted us into His own family, so that the debts are cancelled and His glory inherited. Jesus told Nicodemus, that Jewish religious leader, "Truly, truly, I say to you, unless one is born again, he cannot see the kingdom of God." There are no exceptions. We all must be born into the family of God and begin 'as a little child'.

But we know by our experience and testimony that we have been adopted and scripture affirms it in Romans 8:15, where it says, "For you did not receive a spirit that makes you a slave again to fear, but you received the Spirit of sonship. And by him we cry, "Abba, Father".

So what does adoption teach us? It teaches us that God in His mercy has brought us into His absolute possession. Old life has no more rights over us; God has an absolute right to us. The past is cancelled and its debts are wiped out; we began a new life with God and become heirs of all His riches. Since that is true, we become joint–heirs with Jesus Christ, God's unique Son. That which Christ inherits, we therefore also inherit. Wow! Since Christ was raised to life and glory, we also inherit that life and glory. We are no longer members of Adam's race, of Adam's family. We do NOT belong to him anymore. We belong to the Father.

Yes, we have a new Father. We have a new head of the family. And God the Father loves us and wants us to demonstrate the evidence of our adoption. All of our inherited nature from Adam with its sin and death and consequences has been replaced by an ever developing new nature. Its as if we have now inherited a new DNA from the Father and are beginning to display His nature. Can we say His Divine Natural Attributes (DNA)? What a privilege and honour to be members of this special family and belong to the Father.

Our first identity, as sons and daughters of the Father, has the power to transform us. It is in this relationship that we are made whole by the Father's love. Experiencing His love is so healing. It's in the place of the Father's arms that we feel secure. It's here that He dispels our fears and affirms us.

Such healing from the Father helps us to develop into a mature son or daughter who is ready for love.

Song of Songs 8:4 says "I charge you: Do not arouse or awaken love until the time is right." As we mature within the Father's love we are ready to experience an even deeper intimacy, and our love is aroused. We are ready now for a relationship which is even more intimate and this relationship is with Jesus, Father's own beloved Son. We never stop relating to God as our Father of course and always return to Him to know more of His love but now we are being prepared for something else too. It's for our marriage. This is not a physical marriage to Jesus of course but is a deeper spiritual relationship of intense love and adoraton.

Jesus always knew that we first belonged to the Father before we were given to Him. He knew we were first the possession of His Father. I love the prayer that Jesus prayed to the Father which tells us this. It is recorded for us in John 17:6 "I have revealed you to those whom you gave me out of the world. They were yours: but you gave them to me and they have obeyed your Word." and then in verse 9, "I am praying for them. I am not praying for the world but for those whom you have given me, for they are yours."

Here Jesus makes it very clear that 1) we belonged to the Father first and that 2) we were then given to Jesus. It's at this point that we begin to recognise that the Holy Spirit is taking us somewhere new and on a journey, another journey, a journey somewhere we have not been before and towards someone whom we know but somehow who is now appearing differently than before, who now seems to be showing us that He Himself has another identity. We do know Him as our Saviour ,but there is more.

As we peer through the mists of unrevealed truth we sense He is inviting us to have a far deeper and more intimate relationship with Him than we ever had. Yes, it's Jesus still, but He is no longer just the "Lamb of God who takes away the sins of the world". He is now standing there in the distance waiting for us to follow Him. He's dressed in His Bridegroom apparel with a wedding proposal to make to us and with a wedding invitation in His hand for us. But though this wedding invitation is indeed for you, it is not just for you to attend as a spectator or even as a bridesmaid or the bridegroom's assistant but as His very own precious beloved Bride herself. Yes, we begin to understand, Jesus is also our Bridegroom as well as our Saviour.

The revelation of who Jesus truly is and who we are has been reserved for these end times because Jesus is returning to take us to the Wedding of the Lamb. It's in this season that the Church is receiving this amazing revelation and transitioning in the process.

John the Baptist had to make this transition in his perception of who Jesus was. He too, from seeing Jesus just as the Saviour, had to move on to seeing Him as the Bridegroom. And we the Church, the Ekklesia, need to make that same transition. Jesus will always be the Saviour of sinners but His purpose in being incarnate and going to the cross was to firstly redeem mankind and then to pay the dowry price, the purchase price, with His blood, for the Bride whom He had come to redeem. He truly is our kinsman redeemer.

When we first meet John the Baptist he is preaching His message of repentance and proclaiming the imminent arrival of the expected Messiah. At that time His perception of Jesus was as "The Lamb of God who takes away the sins of the world" John 1:29. You will remember how John addresses Him with these words, as Jesus approaches him in the wilderness area of Judea with a request for John to baptise Him.

Then a few chapters later in John 3:29 John is asked whether he was concerned that another preacher not far away called Jesus of Nazareth was attracting greater crowds than him. John replies that he John is not the Messiah but just a friend of the Bridegroom and later encourages them to go and listen to Him. In so doing he implied that Jesus was the Bridegroom and that John was just the best man. John said in reference to Jesus "the Bride is only for the Bridegroom".

Let's hear His invitation, "Come and I will show you the Bride, the Wife of the Lamb." Let us accept His invitation to "Come up a little higher", to ascend into higher realms of revelation, and to experience deeper moments of intimacy.

Chapter 16: Understanding the Times and Seasons

They were "men of Issachar, who understood the times and knew what Israel should do" 1 Chronicles 12:32.

The importance of this message of the Bride becomes even more significant in the context of the time and season we as His Church are living in. So what is the season and what is the Spirit of God saying to us at this time. If the Church is to cooperate with God in the fulfilling of His eternal purpose then she needs to know what God is saying and doing in our time and our season. We need to be like the Sons of Issachar who as recorded in 1 Chronicles 12:32, sought to discern these things for their day. If God has an eternal purpose and He is moving the world along that prophetic timeline towards that purpose then we must understand where we are along that timeline.

History is His story and is the unfolding of His eternal purpose. Studying history and especially biblical history gives us a better idea of where we are along that timeline. Biblical history records the prophetic words given over time and those that are fulfilled and those that are yet to be fulfilled. Church history is prophecy fulfilled. Prophecy yet unfulfilled is simply that part of Church history yet to be fulfilled. Church history also records the failures and shortcomings of the Church throughout the ages from which we can learn. God is faithful to His Word and His promises and wherever there is error in beliefs or in action He is able and willing to restore and reform.

Studying our history gives us a perspective upon the present and future but I'm aware that not everyone likes history. If you are one of those may I encourage you to still engage with me for we do need to understand the time and season we are living in. The Church is on a journey to discover her true and end time identity and a look back can help us appreciate where we are in terms of the present and the future plans of God.

For our purposes here we are simplifying our view of Church history by dividing it into two periods: the Mortal Church period from its inception to the rapture and then the Immortal Church period from the Rapture and the Wedding of the Lamb to the Millennium Reign and the New Creation. In this chapter we are concerned only to look at the period of Mortal Church history and to do so by dividing it up again into three separate periods called Origin, Decline and Restoration. We are now living in the period of Restoration. God in His mercy and for His own eternal purpose has been restoring to His church that which it had lost since its origination. As we look at these three periods within the Mortal Church history we will see more clearly where we are today in the eternal purposes of God.

1. Origin : The birth of Jesus in Bethlehem.

The prophets had declared that Jesus would be born in Bethlehem in Judea and not in His parents' home town of

Nazareth in Galilee where they were now living. But how could this be? God ordained that in 63 BC Israel would become a part of the Roman Empire and that in the year designated for the incarnation (God becoming man) the Roman Emperor would hold a census and command all people to return to their ancestral home town to register, which in their case was Bethlehem. Mary being very advanced in her pregnancy gave birth to Jesus whilst in Bethlehem.

This was the season of the Lord's appointment and the fulfilment of ancient prophecy. Times and seasons are so important to God. For example nothing could motivate God to send the Messiah until everything was in divine order and the time was right. Jesus came as the "firstfruits of a new race" of those born "not of man's will but of God's", a new human species of Godmen, born of the Spirit with the very nature or DNA of God within them. This would be called the Church race, the Saints, the Ekklesia. Every person born of the Spirit, would be part of this Church race.

Now I don't want to be controversial but we are often taught that the Church was born at Pentecost when the Holy Spirit came upon the disciples in the upper room. The reason for this is that she begins to function as a community of Christ-like, Spirit filled believers, from that point. However. if the Church is the company of those men and women, boys and girls who have been born of the Spirit, that is have received the Holy Spirit, then the Church came into being when Jesus breathed upon the disciples (John 20:22) and gave them authority to forgive sins and said, "Receive the Holy Spirit".

I would suggest that the Church was born on the cross from out of Jesus' side as it were, when the spear was thrown into His rib and blood and water flowed out, two elements always present at a birth. Jesus shed His blood, purchasing the Church who is His Bride, for Himself. The blood was His dowry, Her purchase price. Might it be that the Church, the Bride of Christ, was born out of the rib of Jesus, the last Adam, just as Eve was born out of the rib of the first Adam. The first Adam lost everything that God had prepared for Him: authority, relationship with God and eternal life but Jesus the last Adam won that back for us when He died on the cross. It was at Pentecost that the Church was empowered and found her identity as a community of believers, baptised in His Spirit.

Throughout the first century Christianity spread out from Israel into the Middle East and Europe, Africa and Asia. It was a period of amazing growth and missionary activity. Often this growth was in the midst of terrible persecution yet the Church was vibrant and mission driven. As persecution increased the spread of the faith and as the saints were scattered, signs and wonders followed their preaching. ,"and many mighty things were done at the hand of the Apostles", "and "the Lord added daily to their number those that were being saved" Acts 5:15.

Soon the Church had spread throughout the Roman Empire and beyond. Tradition suggests that the Ethiopian Eunuch of Acts 8 might have been responsible for the birthing of the Church in North Africa. Paul expresses his intention to visit Spain in the Book of Romans. Whether he arrived or not is church tradition but it suggests he did. The Apostle Thomas took the Church to India.

By the end of the second century, Christianity was firmly established in the three continents of Europe, Asia and in Africa. These were the three centres of Christianity for the first 500 years and they developed somewhat independently of each other, each making its own contribution to development of the whole. One of the early Church theologians for example was an African called Augustine of Hippo whose teachings, although not sound in every area, were responsible for giving us much of our doctrine about the Trinity.

2. Deterioration: The Decline of the Church

But what started off as a vibrant supernatural mission Church became by the end of the third century a political and state controlled organisation. By the end the fifth century the Church it seemed had lost the Fivefold Ministry. These were the ministry gifts given to the Church by the ascended Lord Jesus of Apostle, Prophet, Evangelist, Pastor and Teacher. Also it seems that the Holy Spirit's presence had begun to withdraw from the Church. There was still a witness to the supernatural or miraculous of course because God will not be without a witness. People like St Aidan and Cuthbert here in England and St Patrick in Ireland were beacons of light in a dark world but generally the visible Church on earth, by the fifth century had lost much of its power and His presence.

The African Church decline saw the birth and the rise of Islam to fill the vacuum that was created. In 570 AD Mohammed was born and soon Islam moved throughout Africa. The Western Church decline resulted in the 1000 years of spiritual darkness in Europe known as the Dark Ages. The Asian Church however continued undeterred until the Muslim Arabs conquered great parts of India, Persia and Mesopotamia in the 7th century.

3. God's Restoration Programme begins

When Jesus came He created the church and claimed that nothing would stop Him from fulfilling His prophetic declaration, ",I will build My Church and the gates of Hades will not overcome it." Matthew 16:18. However building sometimes has to include restoration and Jesus is committed to restore and mature His Church in order to present Her to His Father as His precious bride. Throughout Church history God has sent seasons of 'refreshings' and 'revivals' to restore Her. These Movements of God were meant to restore or correct the Church and to advance the whole Church towards that maturity that Jesus desires. It was not His intention to create new denominations.

Denominations came about during periods of Church restoration because groups receiving the new truths either were rejected by other churches or became possessive over their own revelation or experience. However from the 1500's onwards God began sovereignly to restore those things that had been lost or corrupted since the days of Origination. Church historians have designated the year

1517 AD as the official beginning of the period of Church Restoration known as the Reformation and since that time there have been five major Church restoration movements.

The Protestant Movement of the 1500's. The Holiness Movement of the 1700's. The Pentecostal Movement of the 1900's. The Charismatic Movement in the 1960's and the Prophetic/Apostolic Movement in the 1980's and 1990's – 2000 onwards.

But perhaps the most significant restoration was the restoration of the Five-fold Ministry Gifts of the Ascended Lord Jesus because as Ephesians 4 tells us, these gifts of Apostle, Prophet, Evangelist, Pastor Teacher were for the maturing of the Church so that the Church/Bride might be ready and without spot or blemish.

In 1525 after the 1000 year reign of darkness in the Western world and in particular in Europe and the decline of the Church in Africa, God declared "Enough is enough" and he began to restore the five-fold ministry that had been lost for so long, back to the Church. It is so interesting to see how God began to restore these gifts of ministry. He did so in reverse order to how they are listed in the scripture because the Church had elevated the Apostle to a position far above the rest. He left the Apostolic ministry, which was considered of most importance, to the last and so He started with the teaching ministry.

Martin Luther, a dis-satisfied Roman Catholic priest had the revelation that we are saved by faith and not by works. As it says in Romans 1:17, "For in the gospel, a righteousness from God is revealed, a righteousness that is by faith from first to last, just as it is written: 'The righteous will live by faith'" Martin Luther and his reformers taught the new truth and this ushered in the Reformation and the Protestant Movement.

So in the 1500's the Teaching Ministry was restored. In the 1600/1700's the Pastoral Ministry was restored as groups of Protestants formed new churches who needed pastoring. In the 1700/1800's the Evangelistic Ministry was restored as many more believers were reading the new printed Bible and were becoming aware of the great commission once again. Missionary movements and organisations were born to take the gospel to all nations. There was the Baptist Missionary Society with William Carey in 1792 and the China Inland Mission in 1865 with Hudson Taylor and the African Inland Mission in 1895 with Peter Cameron Scott.

However there were two remaining ministry gifts that had still to be restored: The Prophetic and the Apostolic. Though all these five gifts were spiritual in nature these last two were dependent on the presence and power of the Holy Spirit in order to operate and be effective. The Holy Spirit however had been grieved and had withdrawn. There had to be a new Pentecost. The Holy Spirit had to know He was welcome again in the Church. In 1906 He came in the form of the Welsh Revival and then the Azusa Street Revival in the USA. The modern Pentecostal Movement was born.

This opened the way for the restoration of the last two ministries but unfortunately those who were baptised in the Spirit at this time soon formed Pentecostal denominations keeping this experience to themselves. It became restricted to the Pentecostal Churches either because of their own possessiveness or because of rejection by more traditional churches. God waited till around 1960 and then He breathed once again and the second wave came which is known as the Charismatic Movement. The final two could now be restored.

In the 1980's the Prophetic gift was restored through the movement known as the Prophetic Movement. The many books and conferences that appeared on the subject of the prophetic at that time bear witness to this. I remember books like 'Know your Prophetic Gift'.

Then in the 1990's the Apostolic Ministry was restored and similarly books and conferences in this decade appeared like 'Know your Apostolic and Prophetic gift'.

By the year 2000 the restoration of the fivefold ministry had been completed and between the year 2000 – 2007 these last two Restorational Movements continued to be established as God 'bedded' these down as it were. Then in the year 2008 many believe the church entered a new 'season'.

The year 2008 is known in numerology as the year of New Beginnings. When, in 2008 in China, the Olympic Games were held, it prompted a response of great national expectation. In China 2008 represented the start of a new era for them since the number eight in their culture also means new beginnings.

Some prophetic voices in the world wide Church have suggested that there was a shift in the spiritual realm in around 2008 and that at that time we entered a season best described as the Season of the Bride. This seems to be a season when God is awakening the Church to understand and embrace her End Time identity as the Bride and is preparing her for her End Time ministry and for the return of Jesus. It is no longer the day of Christian celebrities or megachurch personalities. It is the day of the ordinary person made extraordinary in God as He had always intended it to be. It is a time when every individual believer being filled with the Spirit can rise up in power and authority to do the work of the ministry.

So where exactly are we today in God's eternal programme? I believe that we have been in a season of transition. We are been transitioned from seeing Jesus only as the Saviour to seeing Him as the Bridegroom and ourselves as His precious Bride. All transitions are accompanied by refreshings and revivals. These condition believers throughout the world Church and prepare them to be receptive to the new season of God.

In the past few decades there have seen many major revivals in many parts of the world. There was one in Chile in 1902, then the Welsh revival in 1904, the East Africa revival in the 1930's, the Hebrides Revival UK in 1949, Brownsville or Pensacola USA in 1995, Florida or the Lakeland Revival in

2008, the Bay USA Revival in July 2010, the Dutch Revival starting in 2012 in Hardewijk, Holland and many others that have happened since. These revivals have brought us to where we are now and positioned us for what is yet to come.

But not everyone has heard the voice of the Spirit of God or if they did they have not responded. The move of His spirit in 2008 was heard by only those who were not preoccupied with or blinded by spiritual empire building or mega- church creations. The towers of Babylon were still rising higher. But God is not done. We believe that there is yet the greatest revival coming that will ever have been seen upon the earth. It will come yet before Jesus returns and it will come in the midst of increasing darkness. This will prepare His bride by enabling her to reach her full number and maturity so that she'll be ready for her wedding.

As this time approaches we will become more and more conscious of our Bridal identity. Believers will be driven by a passionate love for Jesus and an intense desire for intimacy with Him as their Bridegroom King. It will be a period of indeterminable length, but will mature us. This will mark both the end of the mortal Church history and the beginning of the immortal Church history when, after the Wedding, we will return to planet earth and will reign here in married partnership with Jesus. It is then that "the kingdoms of this world will become the kingdoms of our God and His Christ".

Meanwhile let's prime our lamps and stay alert.

"Awake, awake! Put on your strength, O Zion; Put on your beautiful (bridal) garments" Isaiah 52:1 (New King James Version).

"Wake up, O sleeper, rise from the dead, and Christ will shine on you." Ephesians 5:14.

Chapter 17: Marriage, the Bride and the Bridegroom as the Central Themes of Scripture

"The kingdom of heaven is like a king who prepared a wedding banquet for his son." Matthew 22:2

It was not long after understanding the importance of times and seasons, that Mike and I saw that the Bride and the theme of marriage was the central theme of scripture. Although Jesus told many parables about a wedding himself, and John the Baptist in the gospels talks about Jesus as the bridegroom, it is in Revelation 21:9 and 19;9, that the Bride of Christ and her wedding known as the Wedding of the Lamb are specifically mentioned and referred to as the event that brings the story of the mortal church to its climax and the story of the immortal church begins.

However I suggest that you will find that the whole of Scripture anticipates this revelation in the final book of the Bible by making Marriage and the Bride its central theme throughout. We discovered that these themes run throughout the whole of the Biblical narrative. The story of our relationship with God, the loss of it and its restoration and our final transformation is set in the context of a marriage relationship.

However scripture itself encourages us to give evidence for the faith or belief that is within us. 1 Peter 3:5 says "Always be prepared to give an answer to everyone who asks you to give the reason for the hope that you have."

So let us now look at scripture and see what evidence there is for deciding whether this is indeed so.

Firstly let's suggest that the Bible has two bookends or covers. The first is in Genesis 2 about a marriage in a garden where we find a bride. The second is at the other end of the Bible in Revelation 19:7 where it says, "for the marriage of the Lamb has come, and his Bride has made herself ready."

Now when we look at the Old Testament we see that the Covenant between God and Israel was a marriage covenant. Isaiah says in verse 5 of chapter 54, "For your maker is your husband, the Lord Almighty is His name, the Holy One of Israel is your Redeemer; He is called the Lord of all the earth."

It is clear from scripture that God intended for His relationship with Israel to be like a marriage. She would be his wife and He her husband. It was clearly a 'Marriage Covenant' that He made because he refers to her subsequent behaviour when leaving Him and going after 'other lovers' (foreign Gods) as adultery.

The prophets always refer to Israel's idolatry as adultery committed against God who is her spiritual husband.

"They committed adultery with their idols," says Ezekiel in Chapter 23 verse 37.

"But you have lived as a prostitute with many lovers," declares the Lord in Jeremiah 3:1. Jeremiah also points to the

Lord as Israel's husband in the following: "Return, faithless people," declares the Lord, for I am your husband." Jeremiah 3:14.

The evidence from the New Testament is perhaps equally compelling.

When we turn to John's Gospel we see in John 2:1 onwards that Jesus begins His ministry at a wedding in Cana in Galilee and that the miracle He performed there, of changing the water into wine was the point at which scripture says, "Here He began to reveal His glory."

In John 1:29 we meet John the Baptist where we find that John's perception of Jesus is as the Saviour. When he first sees Jesus, who comes to be baptised in the River Jordan, John says, "Behold the Lamb of God who takes away the sin of the world."

However in John 3:29 we see that John's perception of Jesus has changed and he sees Him as the Bridegroom. He says, "The bride belongs to the bridegroom. The friend who attends the Bridegroom waits and listens for him, and is full of joy when he hears the bridegroom's voice. That joy is mine." For John the Baptist Jesus was always the Lamb of God but he also sees Him as the Bridegroom.

In Matthew's Gospel we read how Jesus describes Himself as the Bridegroom too. Matthew 9:15 says, "Jesus answered, 'How can the guests of the bridegroom mourn while he is with them? The time will come when the bridegroom will be taken from them; then they will fast.'" Here Jesus clearly speaks of Himself as a Bridegroom.

Then in Matthew 25 we have the well-known parable of the Ten Virgins. It is about those virgins who were either not prepared with enough oil in their lamps and those who had enough oil were not alert or ready as they were asleep when the bridegroom was about to come. It is about being alert and prepared for the return of Jesus and the wedding that awaits us.

St Paul in his letter to the Corinthian Church in 2 Corinthians 11:2 says, "I am jealous for you with a godly jealousy. I promised you to one husband, to Christ, so that I might present you as a pure virgin to him." He knew that his prime responsibility was to prepare the Church as the Bride and to present her to Him without "spot or blemish".

The whole of scripture concludes with the revelation of the Bride and the Wedding of the Lamb. Revelation 19:7 "Let us rejoice and be glad and give him the glory! For the wedding of the Lamb has come and his bride has made herself ready."

And then in Revelation 22:17 we find an affirmation of Jesus as the Bridegroom and an alignment and agreement between the Spirit and the Bride to cry for Jesus to return to take us to that wedding. 'The Spirit and the Bride say "Come!"'

Finally in Revelation 22:20 the Apostle has the last word in scripture and aligns himself personally as part of the bride and cries out "Amen. Come Lord Jesus."

The more I studied about the Bride the more I came to see that accepting our identity as the Bride is not an option. I realised that we must embrace it fully and learn to live as the betrothed for our covenant with Jesus is a Bridal one. For us now, Bridal Identity was not only a biblical teaching or a theology but a paradigm into which everything else must fit and against which everything else makes greater sense. I believe it is the lens through which we must view everything else particularly in these end times as we move closer to the Wedding of the Lamb.

Identity is so important. Knowing who we are makes such a difference. It makes a difference to our motivation and dedication regarding our preparation. It makes a difference to the intensity of our adoration of Jesus, our passion for the things that please Him, our desire for intimacy with Him and our longing for His return.

It makes a difference to our understanding of End-Time events and their chronology because these events can be understood better in the light of the Bridal Paradigm. For me it was not just enough to understand that the Church was the Bride of Christ. I had to learn to think as the bride, behave as a bride, love Him as His bride, intercede as the Bride, serve Him as His Bride.

Knowing the message was not sufficient. We had to get the message. We might 'get' the message but the message had also to 'get' us. The Lord showed us that we enter our bridal identity by faith just like we do our salvation by embracing the truth and confessing that truth because as in all things in the spirit realm, we begin to experience this new identity and its privileges and the new authority it releases when we believe it in our hearts and confess it with our lips.

As we began to confess who we were as the Bride, we grew in confidence in that persona, and fresh revelations and understandings about the bridal paradigm began to be released from heaven. We were conscious that we were now seeing things much more from what we believed was God's perspective and that changed everything.

Chapter 18: The Apostolic and Prophetic Mantle

"It was He who gave some to be apostles, some to be prophets, some to be evangelists, and some to be pastors and teachers," Ephesians 4:11.

It was only after ministering in the nations for several years together, that Mike and I began to recognise the developing apostolic and prophetic nature of our ministry.

The apostolic and the prophetic are two of the five-fold ministries that provide governance and guidance to the Church. The other three are of equal value and importance but demonstrate different expertise and gifting.

An easy way to remember the differences between these five ministries is to describe them this way:

Apostles govern and establish;

Prophets guide and reveal;

Teachers ground and equip;

Pastors guard and encourage;

Evangelists gather and introduce, the gospel.

'I personally started out ministering as an Evangelist, then seeing the state of the broken Body of Christ became a teacher of the Word with a passion for Unity. But then as we began to receive important revelations about the Bride and finding ourselves increasingly desiring that the Church too would understand her own Bridal identity, we moved into an Apostolic/Teaching and Prophetic ministry sharing the Bridal Paradigm.

However we soon realised that this whole 'mandate and ministry' was in a general sense 'Prophetic' in its very nature. It was a John the Baptist mandate, to 'prepare the way for the Lord' and to 'prepare the Bride for her wedding', the Wedding of the Lamb. This was to be done both by teaching and by prophetic declaration and action and by bringing a prophetic Word for the nation and the Church whenever God gave it.

I suppose we should have seen way back in 2010 on a visit to Westminster, London, that our ministry was to be both Apostolic and Prophetic in nature. Something occurred there with the shofar, the Jewish animal horn and musical instrument, with a declaration besides the Big Ben Clock Tower in Westminster that was to be a foreshadow of what was to happen prophetically in many other nations.

I also realise now that the spiritual name given me by the Lord those many years earlier had pointed towards the apostolic/prophetic ministry that Call2Come now has. The full prophetic dimension of that ministry however was to develop gradually because it was quite multi-layered. Mike was developing a very profound gift of prophecy.

As we would prepare for yet another mission trip together, Mike would find himself receiving a prophetic Word for that nation. It was an aspect of the ministry which God was giving to Mike in particular.

However, other expressions of the prophetic began to develop like making prophetic declarations and decrees, or in carrying out prophetic actions with myself blowing the shofar. I could now see how my brass banding experience had prepared me for such assignments. However this development can all be traced back to its beginning with that 'Big Ben' experience in Westminster, London. This is what happened:

Mike and I were invited to take part in an event in London called 'A Call to London'. It was a Prayer, Repentance and Worship event in order for people to gather from across England to make intercession for the city of London.

Mike had been asked to speak about the Bride and I to blow the Shofar. The meeting was good but there was so much happening that the evening over-ran and Mike was offered only ten minutes to speak. He knew he had to decline because he was pregnant with the message and it was not possible to share what he was carrying in such a short space of time. To try to do so would be an insult to the Lord.

The event finished and we walked out of the Emmanuel Centre, Westminster and into the cool air towards the River Thames and Westminster Bridge. We were wondering why we had travelled 300 miles to London from Cornwall and would now have, in my case, to make the overnight journey back only to achieve nothing. Then, as we passed the famous 'Big Ben' clock- tower we looked up at the huge clock face and then back towards each other and we knew why we had come. We were to blow the shofar and make a prophetic declaration to bring an alignment between the time and season of the UK with the time and season of heaven.

It was 11pm at night. The bridge was still crowded with tourists. I blew a long and loud Shofar blast and we declared an alignment in the Spirit. There was a powerful sense of the presence of God hovering over us but not just Mike and myself. Now there were two others who had joined us. We turned around to see two friends of ours also from Cornwall standing beside us and the Holy Spirit said, "In the eyes of two witnesses it shall be established."

This was such a significant prophetic act. The famous clock in London sets its time from that time established at Greenwich Observatory, England. It is known as GMT (Greenwich Mean Time) and every other nation in the world sets its clocks and time based on GMT time in London. Symbolically and in the Spirit realm this was highly significant. What happened that night will have affected things in the UK immediately and would have begun to create an alignment between the plans of men with the purposes of God in heaven.

However because of the significance of Big Ben and GMT for the world, we sensed somehow this act of obedience would also have initiated a shift of alignment in many other nations too, especially as we visited and ministered in the prophetic there and blew the shofar as led by the Spirit.

From this point Mike began to receive more and more powerful prophetic words for the nations the Lord sent us to and we were indeed led to blow the shofar and declare an alignment for those nations just as we had done in London.

This was a pivotal moment in the development of Call2Come. Between us we had so far, separately or together, enjoyed the privilege of ministering in India, Pakistan, Nepal, Malaysia and the Philippines, in Italy and Cyprus in Europe, and in so many different African nations. But the difference now was that each mission took on a prophetic significance and so we would only accept a conference invitation or a visit if we were sure it was of His choice and leading. It had to be specifically in line with what we now knew about our mandate.

Often a mission would also have a specific prophetic assignment. This often involved blowing the shofar but it was becoming as much now about declaring an alignment in the Spirit realm between the Church Bride and the Spirit. Our heart was that 'The Spirit and the Bride would call "Come!"' That alignment and that call would surely indicate that the Bride had 'made herself ready' (Revelation 19:7) and trigger His return.

Mike and myself would always try to go on mission together but occasionally we were assigned to go somewhere separately. One of those occasions for me was quite remarkable and it meant me flying to Israel from Tanzania and back again for one day. It was another assignment with the Shofar but was to be carried out at a high place in Jerusalem and a clock tower in Tel Aviv.

I was about to fly to Tanzania in Africa on my own to fulfil a conference mission trip about the Bride lasting three weeks, but two weeks before I was to fly I was in the presence of the Lord when I clearly heard Him say,

"Howard. I want you to go to Israel and take your shofar. I have a prophetic assignment for you." It was late September 2017.

"Oh Lord, I'd love to go to Israel. When do I go?" I asked.

"In three weeks time," came back the reply.

"But Lord. I'll be in Tanzania then. How can I go to Israel?"

"You can go for a day can't you?" He remarked.

"But Lord I'm 74 years of age (as I was then). Are You asking me to fly from Tanzania to Israel, do what you tell me to do and then fly back to Tanzania all within twenty four hours and then resume my conference programme there?"

Father's response was short and to the point. "Abraham was 75 years old when I called him into ministry. You are only 74."

"What is it you want me to do?" I asked. And He explained it to me.

He wanted me to go first to Jerusalem where He would show me a high place where I was to blow the shofar and declare an alignment between the time and season of Israel with the time and season of heaven. Then I was to travel back to Tel Aviv and meet up below the Jaffa Clock Tower there with several other shofar players from Malaysia who would be in Israel and Tel Aviv for the great Christian Convocation held in Jerusalem each Feast of Tabernacles. There also needed to be at least one Jewish Christian resident of Israel there too. That was important. I was to make all these arrangements and then go. That was it.

But of course I didn't have the finances to go to Israel and there was no natural way for me to get it within the two weeks left. Yet as soon as I agreed to go and stopped arguing I got a phone call from Malaysia out of the blue. It was a Christian friend of mine I'd met the previous year when I ministered in Kuala Lumpur, Malaysia. He was going to the Convocation in Jerusalem though I didn't know it at the time.

He asked how I was and I shared the remarkable conversation I'd just had with the Lord. As soon as he heard he said, "Give me your bank details. I'm transferring the ticket money from my bank into yours now." So some weeks later at the end of the third week of October I flew out to Tanzania and after the first Conference there, took a day out to fly to Tel Aviv, Israel. It was the 1st November 2017. I travelled light since I needed no change of clothing and only my washing things as I would be sleeping both nights on board a plane.

I arrived at 5 am on the 2nd November 2017 in the morning at Tel Aviv Airport and took the shuttle bus to Jerusalem arriving there while it was still early. The Lord had said that He would lead me to a 'high place' where I was to prophesy and blow the shofar but obviously that meant somewhere on the upper hills of the city, so I started walking with my shofar in its bag on my shoulder. I found myself climbing a small road which went past the Garden of Gethsemane.

What a joy it was to be in this wonderful city! Past that place of Jesus' arrest and burial I walked until I saw a sign welcoming me to the Jerusalem House of Prayer some short distance further on. 'Oh how wonderful,' I thought. Could it be here that the Lord was leading me? Was it here that this assignment should take place?

I climbed up the last part of the road and into the entrance of the JHOP and introduced myself and on hearing about my reason for being there they welcomed me to join the Prayer Watch at the top of the building in their prayer tower and carry out the assignment. A little later we climbed the stairs to do just that.

The view from the Prayer Tower was awesome. The circular prayer room had large windows around the room and the view from there overlooked the old City of David and the Kidron Valley. You could raise your hands and pray over large sections of the city from this vantage point.

We worshipped for a while together and His presence was so strong. I then explained the assignment once more to all present and the experience on Westminster Bridge and then blew the shofar and declared what He had instructed me to declare and trusted that this act of obedience would in itself result in the alignment for Israel that He had proposed for that day. Tom and Kate Hess, the directors, were so kind and invited me to spend the rest of the day with them before I set off back to Tel Aviv and the second assignment at the Jaffa Clock Tower.

Some time later in the late afternoon I arrived in Tel Aviv again. Here I met up with my Malaysian Christian friends and the Christian Jewish man who had been invited to join us. It was great to see them all again since I had ministered with them in Malaysia the previous year and after some refreshments together we gathered under the old clock tower in obedience to His instructions.

I explained again to everyone why we were there and what we were going to do but just as I was about to invite everyone to blow the shofars, Pastor Marc Lee, the leader of the group from Malaysia interrupted me and asked if I knew what special day this was that we had gathered together on under the clock. It was actually the centenary of that very day that the Balfour Agreement was signed between Britain and the principal allied powers in which Britain gave support for the establishment of a homeland for the Jewish people in what was then known as Palestine.

This was why we all had to be there. I represented the British and my Jewish Christian friend represented Israel, the people for whom the agreement was made. The Malaysians were there to represent all those who see the Lord Jesus as the Messiah and are awaiting His return to Jerusalem. This is because on the World Prayer Map of the World Prayer Watch, Malaysia is in the prayer sector of nations on that map, which is responsible for the Golden Gate in Jerusalem, which is the gate of course according to Jewish tradition that Jesus will enter as the Messiah and King when he returns to Jerusalem.

On hearing about this centenary day and the fact that we as the British nation had reneged on our promises laid out in that original agreement, I knew I needed to repent on behalf of my nation for this sin and only then could I blow the shofar. In fact we had failed to give over at least 68% of the biblical land promised in the original agreement.

Interestingly, we as the British Empire began to lose much of our Empire from that time onwards, indeed up to about 68%. The Lord says that He will "bless those who bless Israel and will curse those who curse Israel," Genesis 12:3.

So I prayed a prayer of repentance and decreed an alignment between the time and season of Israel with that of Heaven. Then the evening air was pierced by about twenty shofars sounding out a trumpet call to prophesy into place this alignment in the Spirit realm, that the purposes of God and modern Israel would come into line. I then travelled to Tel Aviv airport and flew back to Tanzania in order to continue my programme there.

I was so blessed to discover that only one week later, the then Prime Minister of Israel, Benjamin Netanyahu, was in London meeting Mrs May our Prime Minister that year and the first thing Mrs May did was to reaffirm Britain's support for Israel as a Sovereign nation and express regret at the way we had behaved regarding the fulfilment of the Balfour Agreement. Could it be that that prophetic action in Jerusalem and Tel Aviv contributed towards creating the spiritual climate for such a conversation?

Chapter 19: The Revelation of the Bride and God's Eternal Purpose

Revelation 4:1 "Come up here and I will show you what must take place after this."

Mike and I soon discovered that climbing any sort of mountain whether physical or spiritual had one very interesting characteristic in common. Though a mountain may have one particular summit that is the highest, yet because of the limited view available to the climber as you ascend, it appears that the mountain consists of several summits. Having managed to scale one, you then discover there are more to climb beyond it. And this should not be a surprise to us, since on everyone's journey with the Lord there are numerous 'summits of understanding and revelation' to be received.

I want now to try to carefully describe some more of the precious revelations about the Bride that we received as we climbed further together. Indeed, the immediate benefit of Mike and myself working as one had become very obvious. It intensified our focus and accelerated our 'journey of ascent' and it also enabled us to understand something of what that 'oneness' that Jesus prayed for in John 17 was about. The Holy Spirit was showing us a little more about the corporate nature of the Bride as we worked closely together. We experienced so much synergy and ease of friendship and our sharing and our discussions 'fired off' each other as it were, in understanding new depths of truth. This was a relationship made in heaven.

I'm so grateful to the Lord for this friendship. So I'd like to pay a tribute to Mike here at this point because I want to honour him. I so appreciate his love, his gifting, his wisdom, his deep desire to serve the Lord and particularly his willingness to accept and perfect his prophetic gift, and so much more. I know that I wouldn't be who I am without him. I so appreciate when Mike ministers in the Prophetic.

The prophetic ministry has been so much abused in recent years within the Church.

To exercise the office of the prophet which Mike is called to do is not an easy role to fulfil. It is not just about giving a spontaneous prophetic picture or a short 'word' to someone, although that is part of it, but it is very much more to do with capturing a half-revealed thought, maybe by hearing a few words in your heart, or catching a glimpse of something in your spirit about the spiritual condition of a nation and then researching out that nation's culture, history, religious beliefs and traditions in order to give shape and content to the prophecy that is being awakened within you.

In addition to this, because each phrase and sentence will be recorded and analysed by those who hear it or should be at least, the very imagery, terminology and language of that prophecy must be carefully crafted to reflect the exact expression and intent of the Holy Spirit who is giving it. This is both a learned and practised skill and is the product of a trained and sensitive spirit. It doesn't come easily.

And while we are expressing our appreciations we would also like to give a huge thanks to our dear wives and families who have allowed us to go away on so many occasions in the past twenty years or more, leaving them behind and alone often to await our return, to walk the dogs etc. and maintain the house and home. Thank you Tricia and Jo.

So now, let me attempt to share some of the basic revelations about the Bride that Father was downloading to us at this time and which became part of our core teaching. One of the key revelations we received and shared with each other was that it had always been God's intention to give a precious gift of a bride to His Son. That was always part of His eternal plan and purpose and in my case that revelation came in a question and answer session I had with the Father one morning.

"Father", I asked, "Why did you choose the Jews as Your special people?" It had always fascinated me why He had chosen them and not some other people group. And for what purpose?

His response was both a correction and a question.

"Well Howard. I didn't choose the Jews, I actually created them from the seed of Abraham. But let's pretend that I chose them and you tell me why you think I did and for what reason."

"Whoops. God was asking me that question. I had better think deeply. I didn't want to embarrass myself," I thought.

"Well, You are a God of love and love must be both expressed and received. And it also must be returned. So

You chose the Jews as an object of Your love because of Your need to love and to be loved."

There was a long pause.

"How dare you," He said. "I need nothing. The relationship between Myself and My Son and the Holy Spirit is perfect. I am fully satisfied. We need nothing to complete us. No. I created the Jews because I wanted to demonstrate My love for all to see but more importantly because into the body of one of their seed I would send My Son as Jesus the Saviour, the last Adam, and by spiritual birth and adoption through His sacrifice on the cross I would create from out of His pierced side another Eve, a Spiritual Eve, "not born of the will of man or of the flesh or of blood, but of God," (John 1:13). From these spiritual offspring I would create a bride as a love gift for my Son. It was ever My purpose to do so."

This was a profound revelation and became the foundational understanding of what we called the Bridal Paradigm, that the whole purpose of God's interaction with mankind, Christ's incarnation, man's redemption and transformation, was to form a Bride for His Son.

By becoming incarnate; Christ becoming man in Jesus, He submitted to all the limitations and conditions placed upon the first Adam so that He would experience everything we go through in the physical, mental, emotional, relational, environmental and spiritual realm. He came to suffer death on a wooden cross, an execution so brutal that nothing could surpass it. Philippians 2:8 describes how "He became a man and humbled Himself and became obedient to death – even death on a cross!" and Hebrews 4:15 says that "He has been tempted in every way, just as we are – yet was without sin."

A condition God had placed upon Adam, the first Adam, was that it would be "not good for Adam to be alone" and so He made Mrs Adam inside Adam, of His own DNA, and then put Adam to sleep and brought her out from Adam's rib. She was "flesh of his flesh and bone of his bone." Genesis 2:23

That condition likewise by virtue of Christ's humanity was also laid upon Jesus, the last Adam. So it was not good for Jesus to be alone either and so God always intended to provide a partner, a wife, a helpmate for Him too, made of His substance, born of His spiritual flesh and His spiritual bone. She had to be of His DNA in order to be compatible.

So, just as the first Adam was put to sleep, the last Adam slept for a while in death; "And when Jesus had cried out again in a loud voice, he gave up His Spirit." Matthew 27:50.

At that point a spear was thrust into His rib cage while He still hung on the cross to check whether He was still alive and "blood and water flowed out," see John 19:34. In both Genesis 2:21 and in John 19:34, the same word 'pleura' is used (see the Greek version of the Old Testament known as the Septuagint. In Genesis it is used to describe from where the woman was drawn out of Adam, that is 'out of Adam's rib' and in John it means 'side' as in 'out of Jesus side' and is used to describe from where blood and water flowed, when the spear was thrust into His body.

Blood and water are two elements always found at birth. Could it be that Jesus' Bride was similarly 'birthed' or 'drawn out' of the side of Jesus (the Last Adam) at that moment? Just as the woman was drawn out of the first Adam's side, from 'the pleura', was the Bride in the same way drawn out from there, at the time of His crucifixion?

Was it on the cross that Jesus' Bride was formed within Him and drawn out of Him; bone of His Spiritual bone and flesh of His Spiritual flesh? Certainly it was there that the dowry or Bridal price, which was His blood, was paid. Was His Bride both drawn out from there and purchased there?

Although the Church traditionally teaches that she, the Church/Bride, was born at Pentecost, I am suggesting that maybe she was actually born on the cross out of His side and then at Pentecost she was empowered and began to minister through the anointing and guidance and empowering of the Holy Spirit.

Chapter 20: Jesus Gets Engaged to be Married, Another Bridal Revelation

"It was just before the Passover Feast. Jesus knew that the time had come for him to leave this world and go to the Father. Having loved his own who were in the world, he now showed them the full extent of his love. The evening meal was being served," John 13:1-2.

When we take a conference about the Bride we sometimes like to start one of the sessions by asking the question, "Did you know that Jesus got engaged?" I might challenge them further by suggesting with rhetorical questions that it might have been to Mary, the sister of Martha or Mary Magdalene whom he healed from possession by demons. Having got their attention I then quash any misunderstandings or suggestions of heresy by explaining that before Jesus' arrest in the garden called Gethsemane, Jesus celebrated the Passover Feast with His disciples which is known as 'The Last Supper', but we have come to recognise that this was a Wedding Betrothal supper that He had with His disciples and it was here that Jesus did indeed get engaged. It was to the group of His disciples who were representatives of His precious Bride.

I would like to share now some of the things the Lord showed me from this chapter in John 13 and 14 especially as we compare both the actions and things Jesus said to them, with what is done and said by the husband-to-be at a Jewish betrothal ceremony.

I appreciate that so much in this chapter will contain many personal interpretations of the text in John Chapter 13 and 14 and therefore be very subjective. You might therefore disagree with some things I say but that is OK. It is true that even the phrase "The Lord showed me" is a statement of faith and therefore open to question. Please hear what I have to share and receive what you can.

In John 14 Jesus tells His disciples that He is about to leave them for a while and sensing their anxiety He says in verses 2 and 3, "Do not let your hearts be troubled. Trust in God, In my Father's house there are many rooms (enough room for everyone). If it were not so I would have told you. I am going there to prepare a place for you, and will come back."

Now in Jewish weddings, the betrothal ceremony is where they first pledge their commitment to each other. It is a legal commitment. The public celebration however is the wedding feast which takes place later when the home has been prepared, and the 'consummation' is when they go to their prepared house and enter the marriage bed of intimacy. At the first betrothal or engagement meeting the proposal is made by the bridegroom in which he offers the potential bride a cup of wine but if she refuses the offer of marriage the procedure ends. However if she accepts, then they share the cup together and the bridegroom speaks words of promise and commitment. He then says, "I must go away to prepare a place for you but if I go, I will come again to take you to be with me so that where I am, you will be with me also." Isn't this just what Jesus said to His disciples in these chapters?

In Jewish culture the house that was to be built was usually adjacent to the father's property or an extension to it or was built on the roof and it was the father in fact who took responsibility for the building work not the son. Consequently only the father knew when it was complete and ready for his son to go back and collect her.

As we have seen in John 14 Jesus told His disciples during the Last Supper that He too was going back to His Father but would return again for them. He doesn't however give any indication of when that would be. In fact in Matthew 24, in His discourse with His disciples, He states very clearly that no-one but the Father knows that hour "not even the angels in heaven, nor the Son, but only the Father." Matthew 24:36. This is exactly how it was for a Jewish girl awaiting her fiancés return and is the same for us as His Bride, awaiting His return as our Bridegroom.

There are other interesting parallels of Bridal significance between those things experienced by a Jewish bride to be and those experienced by Jesus disciples during the last supper. In John chapter 13 we find the story of the washing of the disciples' feet that took place that night. John tells us that Jesus "took off his outer clothing and wrapped a towel around his waist, and began to wash his disciples feet," John 13:4-5. Now as part of the wedding preparation a bride would partake of a Mikveh, or a cleansing bath. Mikveh is the same word used for baptism. To this day in conservative Judaism a bride cannot marry without a Mikveh. It is a vital part of her preparation which takes place during her betrothal period.

In the presence of her female attendants the bride takes off her clothes and dresses in a pure white linen dress which her bridegroom has sent her while he is away assisting in preparing the bridal home. Then the young bride steps into a bath of pure water and lays down and submerges herself completely under the water. According to Jewish custom she purposefully opens her toes and fingers to allow the water to touch and cleanse every part of her. Lastly her head is gently pushed under by her attendants. Do you remember that when Jesus gets to Peter and asks to wash his feet Peter refuses and Jesus says "Unless I wash you, you cannot be part of me." Peter eventually replies, "not just my feet but my hands and my head as well!" How significant. Had Peter seen something? Was this Peter's bridal commitment? This was not a washing or baptism for cleansing for as Jesus said "You are washed already". No this was a bridal preparation Mitzvah.

Now it is at this point that I want to suggest that there are hidden treasures to be discovered, regarding the Bride of Christ, by understanding the parallels between Adam, who is referred to as the First Adam, and his bride Eve and that of Jesus, who is referred to as the Last Adam, and His Bride – the Church. Some of this has already been referred to previously but I'd like to give a little more detail here. The Bible tells us that the 'woman' was in Adam and a part of Adam before she became Eve. It is interesting to notice that 'the woman' who eventually became known as Eve, had been formed on the sixth day of creation and was not created as Adam was created but was still part of Adam's body.

Gen 1:27 says, "So God created man in His own image, in the image of God He created him; male and female He created them." Her substance was of Adam. She was made from his rib which had yet to be drawn out of him. She was of the same DNA as Adam. She was also not yet 'Eve' but just known as 'woman'. This is still the case up to Genesis 3:20 when she receives her name Eve, meaning 'the mother of all the living'.The word 'woman' is from a combination of 'wo' which means 'from' and 'man', literally 'from out of man'.

Just as there was a bride within the first Adam, there was a corporate Bride 'in Christ', who was the last Adam also. This has such significance for us as the Church/Bride, the second Eve if you like, for in a sense we were also in Christ, the Last Adam, in the sense that we were in the mind and heart of God even before "the foundation of the earth."

And here is another comparison. Genesis 3:20 described Eve as "the mother of all the living" and Scripture says that the Church, the Bride of Christ, the second Eve, is also the mother of all who are alive in Christ. In Galatians 4:26 Paul says that 'the Jerusalem that is above (the New Jerusalem, prepared as a bride beautifully dressed for her husband – Revelation 21:2) is the mother of us all." Revelation 21:27 says that only those whose names are written in the Book of Life live in the city of the New Jerusalem, which is the Bride of Christ and in Psalm 87:5 it says, "Indeed, of Zion (Jerusalem) it will be said, 'This one and that one were born in Her and the Most High Himself will establish Her.'"

Another interesting parallel is seen in that scripture tells us that woman is the glory of man and so Eve was Adam's glory. Just as Eve was the glory of Adam (the first Adam) so the Church (the Bride of Christ) is the Glory of Christ Jesus (the Last Adam).

I'm sure that Eve was absolutely beautiful. I imagine that she was the delight of Adam's eyes, the fulfilment of all his dreams and desires. I can sense him being so much in love with her and finding such pleasure in just looking at her. She was indeed the glory of Adam.

In the Greek translation of the Bible the Greek word *'doxa'* is used when describing Eve. It means 'glory'. Our word 'doxology' comes from it. It means 'a hymn of praise'. I like that. Eve was like a hymn of praise for Adam.

Paul goes on to say in 1 Corinthians 11:7 that woman is "the glory of man". In like manner the Church, the second Eve, is the glory of Christ in that because of the transforming work in us of His Spirit we "are being transformed into His likeness with ever- increasing glory" 2 Corinthians 3:18. In that sense we are His glory because we are a reflection of His glory. We are His doxology. We are His hymn of praise. Interestingly the same Greek word is used in both instances. That is in Genesis and in Corinthians.

Jesus also delights to look at us and finds great pleasure in us just as Adam did of Eve. Song of Solomon 6:5 puts it so aptly when the King (Jesus) begs the Shulammite girl (the Church/Bride) not to look at Him so intently. He says "Turn your eyes from Me: They overwhelm Me," or as a modern translation puts it, "Do not look at Me like that. You make Me go weak at the knees."

A paraphrase of Ephesians 5:25 – 27 says, "Jesus Christ loved the Church, His Bride and gave Himself to die for her in order to make her holy and pure. He cleansed her with His own blood, washing away every sin which she had committed or would commit. He cleansed her so that He could present to Himself a glorious church, a church full of His heavenly glory. She is now 'without a spot' in His eyes. There is no stain upon her. She is without wrinkles. She, the bride of Jesus Christ which you are a part, is utterly flawless. She is as holy as the face of God Himself and is without blemish."

The Bride is also described as God's masterpiece in creation. Paul in Ephesians 2:10 says, "We are God's workmanship." However the Greek word used here for workmanship is *'poiema'* which means masterpiece. The Lord only has one masterpiece and that is the Bride. We are His finest creation. We are His glory! The church is Jesus' crowning Glory designed to express His own beauty and majesty. Ephesians 3:10 says, "His intent was that now, through the Church (which is His Bride), the manifold wisdom of God (which is His glory) should be made known."

Jesus loves His Church, His Bride, so much and longs to take Her to the wedding, for Jesus yearns for intimacy with His Bride. He desires us to love Him deeply and unreservedly. But in order to gain a Bride He had to pay the dowry price which was His blood. By that blood we became His possession and gained the privilege to reign with Him in the age to come. What glory awaits us! What an honour He bestows upon us! How undeserving His kindness! What an example of His extravagant love for us!

1 Corinthians 6:20, "You are bought with a price. Therefore honour God with your body."

1 Peter 1:18:19, "For you know that it was not with perishable things such as silver or gold that you were redeemed from the empty way of life handed down to you from your forefathers, but with the precious blood of Christ, a lamb without blemish or defect."

Chapter 21: 'Fast' Tracking

Esther said, "Go, gather together all the Jews who are in Susa, and fast for me. Do not eat or drink for three days, night or day. I and my maids will fast as you do." Esther 4:16

When you are about to take a flight in an International Airport, you go to 'Departures' and there you will often find a sign that says 'Fast-tracking this way'. This special entrance enables certain specified passengers to enter and go through the various procedures for security and immigration more speedily.

As Mike and I continued the journey the Holy Spirit was taking us on, we too came to gateways that would accelerate our spiritual progress. We soon discovered that there was a fast-tracking lane opened up for us that would take us further and faster if we chose to use it. It was, to go on 'a fast'.

The Bride will often fast. Whenever we come across a type of the Bride in Scripture we find She often fasts. Esther did for example before interceding as the Bride before the King who was her husband. And there are many different types of fasts, full fasts, Daniel fasts, a day fast, a dry fast, a partial fast, a water fast, an Esther Fast, and many others. But whatever type of fast you take, be sure to expect to fast as part of your bridal journey. And don't be too prescriptive about the nature of the outcomes or results of the fast.

The outcomes of a fast are the Lord's prerogative and are often multi-layered affecting and changing many situations and people. You might have a purpose in mind when you fast but remain open to all other unexpected outcomes. He will surprise you. The Lord said to me one day regarding the consequences of fasting, "Howard, you will sow in one direction and reap in another." This is as true with fasting as it is with sowing finance.

So to encourage you on your journey let me record here one particular Bridal fast the Lord called me to. It was 2004, many years ago now on my 60th birthday. On that day He invited me to celebrate the occasion with Tricia, my wife. Naturally I thought He was going to suggest that I took her out to the theatre or a restaurant for a meal and anticipated several courses of delicious Thai food. I was already drooling at the thought.

"Will you fast for Me?" He asked, "For sixty days. One day for each year of your life so far?"

I was shocked and my jaw dropped open. "What? Sixty days? I'll die!" I cried. "You know when I fast it is totally without food and only occasionally a little warm sweet tea to maintain the fluids."

"Will you Howard? Will you do this for Me?"

The conversation went on for a while until I said, "Well Lord, You know that I love You and will do anything for

You so I will fast for sixty days but may I ask you one request? You know how my fasting concerns Tricia because I tend to lose so much weight and last time when I went on a thirty day fast afterwards Tricia didn't recognise me. Will you promise me that after this sixty day fast I will not lose any weight at all? I know that's naturally impossible but You are the God of the impossible." The deal was struck. I informed Trish and began the fast.

Sixty days is a long time and I had already scheduled to be away on a lot of missions during those months. In fact it turned out to be the busiest time of my life so far. It was 2003. I hadn't met Mike then and was still travelling on my own still. I was in Africa during that period and afterwards in America taking part in a conference in California on Isaiah 19 and the prophecy concerning the end time destiny of Africa (Egypt). After the conference I saw that Benny Hinn was holding a two day series of meetings in Arizona and having tried unsuccessfully to meet him before or even to attend any of his meetings in England, I thought it would be wonderful to stop off on my way home to do so.

In the past I had tried to arrange a meeting with him because I wanted him to pray for me and pass on an anointing for what God was going to do in my life. I'd written many times to make an arrangement to meet him on his previous visits to the UK but without any response. I felt that I needed this in order to establish my ministry but God had other things in mind and important lessons for me to learn. However, my darling wife offered to buy my short air ticket from

California to Arizona and I would pick up my homeward flight to England from there, and fly home via Dallas.

The way God provided transport accommodations and hospitality in Arizona all at the last minute and without any previous human intervention is a miracle indeed but though I was blessed by the meetings and really sensed the presence of the Lord in them, I didn't get to meet Benny Hinn nor receive a blessing from him. I did meet a lovely pastor who was one of Benny's team and chatted with him but nothing more. I was completely confused and utterly disappointed. I was broken. I went back to Arizona International Airport, boarded my plane and sat looking out of the window as we took off watching the desert-like landscape with its cactus trees and parched earth and mountains disappear below. Tears were streaming down my face. I'd come all this way but had not received what I'd come for. It was the 45th day of my fast.

My return air flight for London was to be re-joined at Dallas Airport and I would have about four hours to kill whilst there. It's a huge place laid out in a semi-circular fashion and has a main corridor with the flight bays for each airline and scheduled fight coming off it. As I sat on the plush airport loungers my nostrils caught the smell of, yes steak. Hmmmm! It smelt delicious.

"No Lord. I'm not being tempted now. I know that you can't stop the birds from resting in your branches but you can stop them building nests. I'm on a fast. But you are teasing me. This is Dallas. It's beef territory and it is steak land".

"Have one," the Lord said.

"What? Have what?" I replied.

"A steak." He answered back.

"No Lord, I'm not breaking my fast for anyone," and then I saw the funny side of this contradiction. "I should be begging you to let me have a steak not resisting you for persuading me to break my fast."

His answer was simple but directly to the point. "It is better to obey than to sacrifice."

"You really want me, after forty five days, to have a steak?"

"Well, not exactly, because that smell is coming from outside the airport perimeter but I do have something for you. Just walk around the corridor and you will find it."

So I set off and there around the corridor stood the most attractive advert I could have imagined and close by, a Beef Rib Bar. They were offering freshly grilled fat juicy beef ribs, accompanied with crispy chips, drizzled in tomato sauce and washed down with oceans of ice cold Coca Cola.

Now in England when you order a beef rib you just receive one small rib and some chips served with it. However in the USA when you order a rib you are given the whole rib cage and a mountain of chips to match. It soon arrived and I set to devouring it all and then went straight back into my fast without any indigestion or sickness. It was an amazing meal and so was this whole experience, amazing, because this should not happen. I should have experienced some sort of discomfort but only experienced pleasure and the awareness of having a very full tummy.

I actually fasted for sixty five days during that time because the Spirit led me to eat on four other occasions when we had a visitor for a meal or it was somebody's birthday and when I weighed myself afterwards, guess what? I had lost no weight. I was exactly the same as when I started my fast. And what about the outcomes of the fast? Well, at the end of that year both my children, then in their thirties, came to know the Lord Jesus as their Saviour. The other results of the fast were many, not in the least the changes it produced within me and the difference it made in my relationship with the Lord.

There is a beautiful rider to the experience of attending that Benny Hinn meeting in Arizona. Years later my son and I travelled up from Cornwall to the Excel Conference Centre in London to attend a one day teaching conference on Deliverance by Benny Hinn and his brother. It was well-attended and after the afternoon session we were asked to leave our seats and the auditorium and then to re-enter for the evening session in order to give equal opportunity of good seats for all those who could attend the evening session. My son Jonathan and I came back in as early as we could and managed to get two seats on the left hand side and a few seats back from the front. While we were waiting for things to begin I recognised the pastor I had seen in California from Benny Hinn's team four years before.

"Jon, I'm just going over to that pastor there to say hello again. He is one of Benny Hinn's men. He won't remember me but I met him in California briefly and ought to at least give him my greetings." I was surprised by the pastor's welcome and his obvious joy at seeing me again. "Oh hello Pastor Barnes. How lovely to see you. How are you? Where are you sitting? Oh really. How many of you are there? Let me find you better seats. Please, Come with me." And he took us to two reserved seats just below the rostrum where Benny would be teaching from. Wow! I thought. Maybe some of that anointing will flow over onto me after all. We thanked him profusely and he walked away. But then he came back to us and said, "Howard, I want you on the platform sitting next to Benny."

"W…what? Why?" I said.

"Because the Lord says so. Will you come with me?"

So for the whole of the evening meeting I was sitting with Benny, acknowledging his nods as he taught and facial communications as he turned towards me. It was a wonderful meeting. The power and presence of God was so strong. God

TV was live streaming it all so when I got home again to Cornwall people were phoning me up asking, "What were you doing on God TV with Benny Hinn last night?"

As I drove back with Jon, the five hour car journey, I asked the Lord what all this was about and He reminded me of my motive for trying to see Benny Hinn. I wanted him to anoint me with oil and pass on some of his anointing. Then the Lord said, "Howard. Don't seek a man to anoint you but ask from Me, the Anointer, and don't seek just an anointing but seek the Anointer!"

"And secondly, you were trying to establish your ministry by association with others and by gaining recognition. But see? Do you see what I can do? I arranged all this. Remember I appoint Kings to their places and remove them at My choice. Don't ever try to establish your ministry. It's not yours anyway. It's mine and I will establish it if I choose. Remember when I gave you your spiritual name, I gave you that verse in Zechariah 4:6? This must be the foundation of all you do. "Not by might nor by power but by My Spirit" says the Lord Almighty. This ministry I will raise must not be touched by human flesh or the ingenuity of man because you will be touching the most precious thing that there is, My Bride. So I alone must do it."

It was only as we climbed further up the Mountain of Myrrh did we understand how precious to Him is His Bride. She is the most precious of all His creations. She is His glory and

He had said, "I will not share My glory with another." He is indeed jealous and very protective over her.

Chapter 22: By Royal Appointment Divine Connections

'While they were worshipping the Lord and fasting, the Holy Spirit said, "Set apart for me Barnabas and Saul for the work to which I have called them." Acts 13:2

"And we know that in all things God works for the good of those who love Him, who have been called according to His purpose." Romans 8:28

As Mike and I continued the journey and to visit more nations, the difficulty of our climb varied as the terrain changed and the spiritual weather and atmosphere altered, just as it does in the physical dimension. We knew the Lord had called us to bring this Bridal message to these nations but at times we were very conscious of the infertile nature of the church soil in the nation we were visiting. By church I mean the national church rather than any individual church. Of course some individual churches were very open to the Spirit and eagerly accepted our Bridal message and wanted more and more teaching. Others were very cool, even resistant and not at all interested. But our main desire was to discern the spiritual temperature of the national church itself.

From the onset of planning a new mission we would earnestly seek the Lord for His revelation about the state of the Church within that nation in order to understand the spiritual condition of the physical nation itself. The condition of any physical nation will be very much affected by the condition of the Church, within it. The 'spiritual nation' as the bible calls it, must come into alignment and agreement with Heaven first and then we can defeat the spiritual rulers and their kingdoms that attempt to rule or influence the physical nation, its governments, politicians, and leaders of all the different spheres of society.

Mike's prophetic gift was so valuable in this respect and was being finely tuned. He would seek the Lord for a precise prophetic Word to give to that nation and whilst there we would often seek Father's permission to open a court in Heaven. We sensed that this prophetic word and any proclamations following it were to be declared both in heaven and upon the earth. I cannot explain how we were aware of this but that is what happens in the prophetic realm. You sense it in the spirit and have the choice to follow through in faith or not.

If we sensed that Father was leading us by His Spirit and has granted us permission, we would open the court with the blowing of the shofar and maybe we would anoint the ground with oil. Then Mike would speak out that prophecy and as the Spirit led we would decree and declare anything the Spirit led us to pronounce. Most times this was done at the main conference but sometimes beneath a significant clock tower in that particular nation or outside a public building of governance. Many many times and often within a few weeks after that act of obedience something quite significant would happen in either the political, economic or cultural/social arena. There was always however some sort of shift in the spiritual temperature or atmosphere of his Church there.

It is amazing how much this spiritual atmosphere varied from nation to nation. Just as the physical climate differs from nation to nation and even within the same nation, so does the spiritual climate vary. Some nations feel heavy, dark and oppressive and are resistant to the Holy Spirit. As our spiritual sensitivity developed we could discern any demonic strongholds more readily and subsequently any positive spiritual shift. When the spiritual opposition was heavy we would then draw closer to Him for He was our shield and protector.

Sometimes the oppression was so heavy we almost found it hard to breath in the Ruach or Breath of God, so we would need to breath deeper. It was the same as we pressed in to experience fresh encounters with Jesus our bridegroom. Our personal journey was always about seeking to "Come up a little higher" and just as the air higher up a mountain gets thinner so the higher we climbed on our journey the rarer the spiritual oxygen became and the greater the need there was to manage His supply by abiding in Him. Because His Holy Spirit was the air our spirits breathed, we soon learned to take long deep breaths in the Spirit.

We also learned that loving one-another was not an option but a command. If there is no love between us as brothers then not only were we living in sin and disobedience but God could not abide with us. Scripture tells us that we demonstrate our love for God when we love one-another. It was so important that Mike and I walked in humility together and respected and honoured each other and dwelt in love.

I shall never forget the prophetic experience I had in Pakistan years earlier when ministering there, way back in around 2004. A great many believers worship together in small groups in their homes because of the difficulties of having public church buildings in a Muslim society. I was meeting with a House Church and we were worshipping together. I became aware that the Lord was wanting to speak through my mouth in a word of prophecy so explained to everyone that I was going to begin with the thought in my heart and see where it went from there.

The Lord began to say, "Did you know there is air in Heaven and that the air of Heaven is love? Did you know that I breathe in Heaven? I breathe in and I breathe out. I breathe in, love and I breathe out, love. But did you know that sometimes I want to come and spend time with my children on earth but I cannot come. That's because I would not be able to breathe; I would suffocate. That is because there isn't enough love in the atmosphere."

The Lord is very strategic so we knew that He had a plan for us as we visited any particular nation and a strategy to follow in order to discover that plan. We soon recognised that the Father had plans and schedules and that He moves in seasons and is meticulous about His timing. I love the verse in Galatians 4:4 which says, "But when the time had fully come, God sent His Son, born of a woman."

God began to show us that there was a particular way He wanted us to enter a new nation and a particular 'Gate of Entry' He wanted us to use to gain access.

Of course sometimes we would minister in a nation in response to an invitation sent to us and which after much prayer we had sensed was His will for us to accept but most times it would begin by sensing a 'nudge' in the Spirit, a burden in our heart for a particular country. Then having discussed it together and researched about the nation, its history and spiritual background etc., we would then ask the Lord to link us up with someone in that nation whom He had been preparing and who was becoming Bridal- conscious.

Usually this person would not only be a pastor but also an intercessor and was a part of the prayer movement in that land. Gradually this became so much the norm that we would then understand that it was part of His strategy since if anyone was to be found who should be sensitive to what the Spirit was saying to the Churches in this hour, then they ought to be found from amongst the intercessors. These are those who seek to share the burden of Father's heart and align themselves with His Spirit.

It had been that way with our connection with Kenya. Both Mike and myself had had a long mission history with Kenya and in fact it was one of the first nations we travelled to together. But through a developing link with Intercessors for Kenya (I4K) we were led to travel to Nairobi to discuss together the possibility of holding an 'Awakening the Bride' Conference with I4K in Nairobi, the capital of Kenya, in February 2017. It was a relationship arranged in Heaven.

We decided to meet with the leaders of I4K and so arranged for the provisional discussion meeting to be held at a hotel in Nairobi. I flew in and was met by Pastor Benson Nyangor of I4K and taken to the hotel. However the choice of hotel that Benson made was highly significant. It was at the Hadassah Hotel.

Hadassah is the Hebrew equivalent for Esther and she was the Jewish Queen and bride of the King of Persia who interceded for her people throughout the Persian Empire and saved them from annihilation. Esther is a type of the Bride of Christ in terms of her intercession, delegated authority and gracious character. Later when Pastor Benson saw the significance of the choice he had made, but without realising it, he was so much encouraged.

The meeting went very well and the Bridal Conference was agreed and plans drawn up. Apostle Phoebe Mugo, who chaired the meeting and was the overseer of I4K shared with us how the Lord had for many years been speaking to her about the Bride and had given her dreams and visions about these things. Truly the Lord had gone ahead of us. How precious it is to walk in His ways!

The conference was called "The 2017 Church Ministers' Apostolic – Prophetic Conference" with the theme *Kenya's Season for Bridal Awakening.* It was to be held in a hall, non-other than McBride's Hall, at Christ is the Answer Ministries (CITAM) Church, Nairobi. Please notice the word 'Bride' in McBride!

I call these 'God's gems of coincidence or convergence'. These are His kisses of confirmation. He doesn't have to do these things but does so as acts of His love to demonstrate His presence and pleasure.

Other nations were now being connected to the ministry of Call2Come. It was clear that God was developing a network of nations who were chosen to carry the Bridal Message: Call2Come Malaysia under Pastor Roy Mattiah and Intercessors for Malaysia (I4M); Call2Come India under Reverend Prinson Chacko; Call2Come Liberia and I4L under Dr George Zorbah; Call2Come Nepal under Pastor Dhan Lama and Call2Come Japan under intercessor Akemi Priscilla.

We wish we had space to name all of the leaders here because we appreciate them so much. We bless them all for their commitment and dedication in serving our Lord though this movement. However, we would want to stress once again that Call2Come is not so much a ministry as a 'movement' of God in our time. It's about a message, the Bridal Message, and the return of Jesus. The ministry is but a vehicle to carry the message.

Although God is so faithful, sometimes His timing and schedules are much more elastic than ours and His plans take much longer to establish than that which we would sometimes anticipate or hope. Sometimes a plan or arrangement He has, takes such a time to conceive, to gestate and to birth. However it is always worth the wait. Some of our 'divine connections' took many, many years to mature. Here is a wonderful example of this. It is a testimony of God's wonderful grace.

Between 2003 and 2005 I was feeling very burdened for the islands of the Caribbean like Haiti, Dominican Republic and Cuba, especially Cuba. I had been writing to several pastors in these islands over a long period of time. I had also built a relationship with a wonderful man of God, a Pastor Alvaros Berios from Nicaragua, a nation in the most southern end of Central America near to the Caribbean. He had written to ask me to join him on a mission to Colombia in Latin America. It was as if God was beginning to open up the Americas for the message of the Bride.

But these communications also fired up in my spirit a real desire to find a genuine 'divine connection' with Cuba too, which was another Spanish speaking nation. I decided to write to a pastor from there who had written to me on Facebook once or twice, to see how that relationship might develop, though I had little knowledge about him. Yet his name was so impressive in my spirit that I accepted that it was God's leading so I sent a message to him.

Cuba I knew was a Marxist socialist country and had under Fidel Castro's leadership experienced a revolution which set its course in an atheistic communist direction. From that moment the Church there was to suffer repression and persecution.

My communications with Pastor Maikel were very slow at first because of that nation's very limited use of the internet and poor mobile network infrastructure. Mike and I both felt however that Cuba was strategic in God's eternal purposes especially because of her links to Africa as a staging post in the Great Slave Trade and God's redemptive plans for her. I wrote to Maikel asking him about the possibility of us being granted a Religious Visa for a mission there as I knew that you needed that since Cuba was a Marxist nation. It took ten years of communication on social media to get that Religious visa.

Divine connections are indeed 'Divine'. They are not of man but God obviously uses man to send the emails, search for possible links if you like and to communicate via WhatsApp or Facebook Messenger. The secret is in discerning when your persistence is coloured by your own enthusiasm or vision and is not of Him. Persistence and determination are necessary but it's knowing when to desist and when to persist and to recognise that a particular avenue is not of His making.

But God's timing is perfect and His Divine connections are truly 'Royal Appointments'. We eventually went to Cuba after about ten years of planning and praying and we had an amazing time of teaching and prophetic ministry there. It was so good to meet these precious men and women of God and their fellow Pastors with whom we had been communicating for so long. They all so eagerly embraced the Bridal Message and Paradigm.

Subsequently we were able to establish Call2Come Cuba under the leadership of Pastor Maikel Perez and his friend and fellow pastor, Pastor Markos Perez and create a prayer network called Intercessors for Cuba (I4C) overseen by another Cuban servant of the Lord and friend of theirs, Abel Velazquez Infante. Cuba is now one of these leading shofar nations within the Call2Come Movement. But why was this connection so amazing? Well, you remember that I had very little information as to who Pastor Maikel Milan Perez was when I first contacted him.

We trusted the Lord to connect us to men or women of influence so that they in turn can influence others with the message we bring and so affect change. But when we finally met Maikel we heard that as a younger man he was none-other than the leader of Fidel Castro's Communist Youth Movement but who had been wonderfully saved. We were so impressed and blessed. God does all things well. These men now head up the Holy Spirit Renewal Movement in Cuba and the Intercessors Prayer Movement in the land. Maikel is indeed a man of great influence in the nation. He and Pastor Markos continually need our prayers.

As already mentioned in this chapter and stated clearly in the next, God is a remarkable strategist. So it wasn't long before the Lord gave a vision to Mike called 'The Seven Shofar Vision' about seven angels and seven shofars and this vision helped us to prioritise in line with His plans and programme, the nations we were to visit over the next few years.

Chapter 23: Our Heavenly Father is the Chief Strategist – The Shofar Vision

"The LORD said to Moses, "Say to the Israelites: 'On the first day of the seventh month you are to have a day of rest, a sacred assembly commemorated with trumpet (shofar) blasts. Do no regular work, but present an offering made to the Lord by fire.'" Leviticus 23:24-25

The shofar is a Jewish instrument. It is an animal horn which when played as if it were a trumpet sounds an alarm or heralds the arrival of a king. It is also an instrument of celebration and declaration. However for us at Call2Come it is also a very prophetic instrument and whenever played under the anointing invokes, we believe, the presence of God and opens a portal into heaven. We also believe that its sound is granted the power to establish that which has been decreed. We have found that it also imparts a blessing and releases an anointing for revelation upon those who desire it and have faith to receive it. I appreciate that this is our understanding and experience and doesn't have any specific scriptural foundation.

We believe that when it's blown over a nation, in faith and under His anointing, it announces over that nation, in the Spirit realm, the Lord's desire to bless. It begins to prepare the people's hearts in order to receive that blessing and also activates an alignment between the time and season of that nation with the time and season of Heaven.

However, a 'Shofar Nation' is a nation which is chosen by God to carry specifically the Bridal message to the Church in that nation and to other nations as the Lord leads them

God was gracious to give Mike a prophetic vision about the significance of the Shofar and about a Shofar nation. This prophecy not only reflected the strategic nature of our God but provided for us a mission plan and schedule which continues to be implemented even to this day.

The Prophetic Vision:

"I saw the Lord seated on his throne of great glory surrounded by angels and on the clouds. Then the clouds divided over the land of Kenya and I saw that one of the angels was holding a great shofar and the shofar was given to the watchmen on the walls of Kenya. And I heard a voice proclaim "blow the trumpet and sound an alarm on my holy mountain."

And I asked the Lord about the shofar and he said,

"Let my people called by my name who have ascended the mountain on which I have revealed my end time purpose blow the trumpet for the time has come to sound an alarm. I am coming soon."

The Lord said "Kenya is the lead shofar nation in Africa. This not only means literally blowing the shofar but she is chosen to share the End Time message of the Bride and One New Man to the nations of Africa and beyond. Through her I will breathe my Spirit so that the trumpet blast will sound by my Spirit through her mouth."

And I understood that there were still other shofars to be given to places upon the earth but I did not know where. Then I marvelled at the great mysteries of heaven being given to mankind in this day and praised His holy name." (End of vision.)

Two other nations were named at this time and these were the UK and Israel, though Israel would be the last to embrace it. The vision didn't reveal the location of those other shofar nations but we knew that there were seven key shofar nations that the Lord wanted to show us.

Through prayer, the following nations were selected and represent those seven we sensed might be the nations where shofars are to be blown. They are the nations being prepared to both hear, receive and then share the end time message of the Bride and the One New Man and to announce the return of the King. However, discerning this list is an ongoing process and the final list of the first seven shofar nations is yet to be confirmed. The reason that there are four nations from Africa is because of Africa's special role in the fulfilment of God's End-Time purpose as revealed in Isaiah 19.

The list of nations:

1. The UK, who has an Apostolic, Prophetic and missional mandate amongst the nations. She has a governmental and legislative gifting. She is chosen to initiate a new global movement to Awaken and Prepare the Bride and to see her cry 'Come Lord Jesus Come'

2. Kenya represents Africa at the East African Gate. She contains the Ancient Wells which must be reopened. It is an Islamic portal which will facilitate the return of Ishmael as does the nation of Egypt. It also carries an intercessory office. She will carry the shofar bridal message to her East African neighbours but also has an apostolic responsibility over all of Africa. She is a lead shofar nation.

3. Liberia which is at the West African Gate. She speaks of Redemption and Freedom. Though hidden at this time she will rise up and fulfil her destiny amongst the nations and take the shofar message throughout West Africa.

4. South Africa is the Southern African Gate. She too has a specific redemptive calling for Africa. She carries the shofar to the southern African nations.

5. Egypt is the North African Gate. She will participate powerfully in the restoration of Ishmael and help build that 'Highway to Assyria' spoken of in scripture. Isaiah 19. She will be a 'Blessing upon the earth'. God is so grateful for her grace that has shown towards Israel in particular for sheltering His Son in the days of Herod.

6. Cuba. The Caribbean outpost. She has a special place because of her connection as a staging-post for Africa in the days of her slavery. She is part of Africa's salvation and the fulfilment of Africa's destiny. Also the Isaiah 19 prophecy. She is also called to blow the shofar, to bring the Bridal message to Latin America and all Spanish speaking nations.

7.   Malaysia. The South East Asian Gate. She represents the Golden Gate sector on the map of the World Wide Prayer Watch and guards in the Spirit that gate always calling on the Messiah to Come! She shall be known as The Guardian of His 2nd Coming and is a catalyst for revival in S E Asian Nations. She carries the Bridal shofar to S.E. Asia.

We believe that there other nations yet to be given shofars. The Holy Spirit will reveal these when the time is right. Each of these Bridal Nations will have the authority to blow the shofar under a prophetic Bridal anointing and their mandate will include awakening and preparing the Bride in their own nation and to take it to their neighbouring nations.

One day there will be a body of believers representing the Bride in every nation, for we know that this is the message that the Spirit is bringing to the Churches today.

The Significance of Israel:

Israel is a key shofar nation but we believe will be the last shofar nation and distinct from all previous nations. Her shofar assignment will be different to the others.

When the Bride of Israel blows the shofar it will unite all the shofar nations together and amplify the shofar sound from them as one sound. This sound will rally the Bride upon the earth to cry out the final Call to Come and this final shofar 'Call', coming out of Israel, will welcome the Messiah. It will herald His arrival.

We pray that sometime soon the Bride in every nation along with Israel will hear the Spirit's cry and recognise His voice and reply together in response, "Come, Lord Jesus Come! Maranatha. Let the Spirit and the Bride say Come!"

Chapter 24: The Authority of the Bride

"He called his twelve disciples to him and gave them authority to drive out evil spirits and to heal every disease and sickness." Matt 10:1."Then the king extended the gold sceptre toward Esther and she arose and stood before him." Esther 8:4.

We have seen that the Wedding of the Lamb is the central event of Church history and the Church/Bride and her Bridegroom are its central characters. The Bridegroom has all authority but has chosen to share it with His Bride and it's after that wedding that this authority begins to be fully demonstrated as the marriage covenant between them is ratified.

The bible describes two periods of Church History: Mortal Church history and Immortal Church history. Mortal Church History describes that period when the Church is on earth and is made up of mortal beings or human beings. It ends with our rapture and transformation into immortality. Immortal Church History describes that period of Church history when we have become immortal and have received our resurrected bodies. It begins with our return to earth for the millennium reign.

The fulcrum point or the transitional event between these two periods is the Wedding of the Lamb. The Wedding of the Lamb is all that Mortal Church History is leading up to and all that Immortal Church History is leading off from. It's then that we are made totally like Him and are fully compatible to Him. "In a flash, in the twinkling of an eye, at the last trumpet. For the trumpet will sound, the dead will be raised imperishable, and we will be changed.

For the perishable must clothe itself with the imperishable, and the mortal with immortality. When the perishable has been clothed with the imperishable and the mortal with immortality, then the saying that is written will come true: 'Death has been swallowed up in victory.' " 1 Corinthians 15 :52 – 54.

If this is such a focal event, and it is, then the Marriage of the Lamb and our position as His Bride is of infinite importance and our preparation to 'make ourselves ready' for it is so vital. Part of that preparation is to fully embrace our Bridal identity and aspire to live in the fullness of being His Bride, even now!

Earlier I said how concerned I was when people relegate the message about the Bride to just another theology. Bridal Identity is not only a biblical teaching or a theology but a Paradigm into which everything else fits and against which everything else makes better sense. It is the lens through which we can view everything else. Knowing who we are makes such a difference. Knowing that we are to be His bride and are getting married makes a difference to our motivation and dedication in getting prepared for that wedding. It also makes a difference to the intensity of our love for Jesus for our love has been not only aroused but our passion for Him and for the things that please Him have become our deepest longing. We find our desire for intimacy with Him has intensified and we long for His return.

It also makes a difference to our understanding of end-time events and their chronology because these events and their order of fulfilment can best be understood in the light of the Bridal Paradigm. Who is the bride, is she both Jew and Gentile, and if so when will Israel be saved? Where is she at the time of consideration in terms of being still on earth or whether she has been taken to be with the Lord in Heaven? These are questions which help us sort out the chronology of events.

So our bridal identity is of much importance and we must learn to embrace it.

Although I've said it before, allow me to say it again: we must learn to walk in the full identity of who we are. It's not enough to just understand the Church as the Bride. We must think like the Bride; behave like the Bride; love Him as His Bride; intercede like the Bride. Knowing the message is not enough. We must become the message.

But the Bride is a wonderful creation for she is neither singular nor plural but corporate. There is only one Bride and not several Brides. It is true that the other metaphor, that of the Body of Christ, that Scripture uses when referring to the community of believers is also about oneness but is used to emphasise the unity between its members and the need for each to operate cohesively as one body, each member functioning in his or her particular gifting. However this metaphor of the Bride goes further than this for me. It is not about function but about identity and personhood and relationship with Jesus as a living being. She IS His Bride and as such enjoys a corporate nature. This identity of being the Bride of Christ gives her the grace of a greater authority because as 'one' joined together in marriage her husband authority is delegated to her by her husband, the Lord Jesus. It is indeed a mystery.

The corporate nature of the Bride was to me an amazing revelation.

The word corporate is from Latin corporātus which means made into a body, from corporāre, from corpus, made into one person. The Bride can never ever exist as a singular person, nor can she be only plural as in a company or a group of believers but she is at all times corporate. She exists as a created corporate being. She is a reflection of her Bridegroom who Himself can never be singular (as in separate from) but is part of the corporate Godhead. They are three in one and one in three persons. Living and loving and moving together in perfect harmony and, in showing the utmost honour and respect for each other, they demonstrate what Jesus meant in John 17:21-23 when He prayed for us that we as believers would be 'One'.

One day the Lord showed me that there were three increasing degrees of authority given to us by God, from singular to corporate and the Bride enjoys the highest form of these three. There is Singular authority, Plural authority and Corporate authority. I first received this revelation when I was preparing to minister one day whilst in Cuba. The Lord told me He wanted me to teach about the authority He has given us as believers but then He showed me that there were three levels of authority that we could experience. However before I share these, I want first to explain the difference between authority and power.

The Greek word translated as 'authority' is 'exousia,' and its basic meaning is to have the right to rule or govern, as one whose will and commands must be submitted to and obeyed.

The second Greek word 'dunamis' is translated as 'power'. It means to have an inherent strength, power, or ability to bring about a desired purpose. The distinction between the two words is not always made clear in the Bible. The King James Version sometimes translates both 'exousia' and 'dunamis' as "power" as it does for instance in the King James Version of this verse: "Behold, I give unto you power to tread on serpents and scorpions and over all the power of the enemy." (Luke 10:19). A persons 'power' resides very much with the one exercising that power. It resides in their strength of body, strength of their mind or wisdom or influence.

Our 'authority' however does not depend on our own ability or on the merit of the person exercising that authority because it's always delegated. It is given from one to another to act on their behalf and the more authoritative is the one who delegates, the greater the influence that person has to whom it is given. They are acting only as a representative of the other on their behalf and on their authority but share that authority absolutely and unquestionably.

I heard a story that illustrates the differences between power and authority so well and will share it here. I trust it will help. There was, in a certain town, a young woman police officer who was quite short in stature and build. She was always immaculately dressed in her pure white shirt and blue tie, dark-navy skirt or trousers and shiny black mirror-like shoes. She was a faithful and reliable officer and took her job very seriously.

One day she was parked in her patrol car at the end of a road junction keeping her eye on all the traffic when suddenly she spotted in the distance a huge heavy lorry enter the one way road the wrong way and begin to travel at speed towards where she was parked and where the road bent sharply. She knew that the traffic around that bend would soon be released by traffic lights and enter that road in the opposite direction and that there was the high probability of a head on collision as these vehicles sped towards each other.

So without any concern for her own safety she started her motor and came out from the corner of the side road and as fast as she could drove toward the approaching lorry ahead of any traffic behind her.

When she was a short way up the main road she rammed on her brakes, jumped out and stood defiantly a few paces in front of her car. As the lorry sped towards her she raised her arm and with an outstretched palm pointing towards it she cried, "Stop in the name of the Law!" There was a screeching of brakes and the smell of rubber but eventually this huge truck shuddered to a stop in front of her. Though the lorry was far heavier and faster and more powerful than her, she had the authority.

The devil may have power but he has no authority given him by God but only that handed over to him by sinful man. Jesus has delegated authority to His disciples and especially to His Bride because of her understanding of who she is in relation to Him.

So what are these three levels of authority? There is Singular Authority as a single believer: Matthew 10:1: "(Jesus) called his twelve disciples to him and gave them authority to drive out evil spirits and to heal every disease and sickness." There is Plural Authority as a group of believers: "Again I tell you, that if two of you on earth agree about anything you ask for, it will be done for you by My Father in heaven." Matthew 18:19. This prayer is often referred to as the 'Prayer of Agreement'. And there is Corporate Authority as with the Bride. The reason why the Bride has the highest authority is solely because of *who* she is and *whose* she is and because of her corporate nature. So who is she and whose is she?

"One of the seven angels who had the seven bowls full of the seven last plagues came and said to me, 'Come, I will show you the bride, the wife of the Lamb.'" Revelation 21:9. She is the Lamb's wife. That is who she is and as such belongs to Him. She is one with her Bridegroom and consists of His substance. She is many persons in absolute oneness with each other in substance and in being, formed by God, a person most beautiful, made of His spiritual divine natural attributes.

As said already the Bride is not just a group of individual believers working together in unity and agreement but is a corporate being and is being transformed moment by moment by the Spirit to become totally compatible with Him. As it was with the first Adam and Eve so it is with the

Bride and her Bridegroom the last Adam. Eve was entirely compatible with Adam because she had been created from him and was of his substance. So likewise the Bride must be and <u>will</u> be totally compatible with Jesus if She is to be His Wife. One day, as promised in scripture when, "in a flash, in the twinkling of an eye, we will be changed" and that process will be complete. 1 Cor 15:52. Meanwhile as His betrothed we must "reckon ourselves crucified with Christ" and continually "put on the new nature" and put off the old.

However, we believe that even now while this process continues, we as the Bridal company, like Esther who is indeed a type of the Bride, can learn to exercise (though in part) her delegated authority and enter our heavenly Father's Court and intercede like Esther did. We can have confidence that our Father, the Judge of all men, will grant us favour to bring our requests to Him and believe that He will extend the golden sceptre towards us. Amazing! And all this is because of who we are and whose we are as His Bride. We are His possession bought by His blood and as such, we belong to Him. In His grace He has granted us to share authority and to sit in heavenly places with Him. Yes, it's all of grace! Amazing Grace!

But there is another place in the Spirit realm where we have authority to rule and to judge and proclaim and its once again only because of who we are in relation to the Bridegroom as His Bride. And this is at the 'Gates of the city'.

Chapter 25: Bridal Authority at the Gate

"And they blessed Rebekah and said to her, "Our sister, may you increase to thousands upon thousands; may your offspring possess the gates of their enemies." " Genesis 24:60.

Not only does the Bride have access like Esther to enter and intercede in the Courts of the King but she exercises authority at the 'gates of the city' as well. Let me explain.

Gates are very symbolic and significant. The Bible shows us clearly in the Old Testament that the vulnerability and strength of a fortress or stronghold always rested in its gates. We have the image of a stronghold surrounded by thick walls, a drawbridge, and fortified gates.

However, the gates of the ancient cities were not as we imagine today's gates to be; they were massive gates made of stone, iron, brass, or wood frequently sheeted with metal. They were tall and wide, the 'Beautiful Gate' of Herod's temple (Acts 3:2) was made of brass and required twenty men to close it. These gates were opened during the day to allow the citizens to come and go, but were generally closed and barred at night as a safety measure to keep out enemy attacks.

The gates were shut at nightfall (Joshua 2:5) because they were the chief point from which the enemy attacked (Judges 5:8). Whoever controlled the gates of the stronghold ruled the city. To control or 'possess' the gates meant you had authority and control over the city. All sorts of activities went on at the gate of the city, not all positive. Idolatrous acts were performed at the gates (Acts 14:13) so that sometimes it was necessary to cleanse the gates.

Battering rams were set against the gates (Ezekiel 21:22) and for an enemy to destroy a gate was to underline the totality of a victory. Nehemiah emphasises this when he records that the gates were broken down and burned with fire (Nehemiah 1:3). They were utterly destroyed. The gates were seats of authority (Ruth 4:11). At the gates wisdom was uttered according to Proverbs 1: 21. Judges and officers served at the gates administering justice (Deuteronomy 16:18), and the councils of state were held at the gates (2 Chronicles 18:9). Public announcements would be heralded there. Often the scriptures were read at the gate (Nehemiah 8:2-3), and the prophets proclaimed God's message from the gates (Jeremiah 17:19-20).

The first mention of a city gate is found in Genesis 19:1. It was at the gate of Sodom that Abraham's nephew, Lot, greeted the angelic visitors to his city. Lot was there with other leading men of the city, either discussing the day's issues or engaging in important civic business. In the Law of Moses, parents of a rebellious son were told to bring him to the city gate, where the elders would examine the evidence and pass judgement (Deuteronomy 21:18-21). This affirms that the city gate was central to community action.

Another important example is found in the book of Ruth. In Ruth 4:1-11, Boaz officially claimed the position of kinsman-redeemer by meeting with the city elders at the gate of Bethlehem. There the legal matters related to his marriage to Ruth were settled. As Israel combatted the Philistines, the priest Eli waited at the city gate for news regarding the ark and to hear how his sons fared in the battle: 1 Samuel 4:18.

When King David ruled Israel, he stood before his troops to give instructions from the city gate (2 Samuel 18:1-5) and after his son Absalom died, David mourned but eventually returned to the city gate along with his people as this would be a sign to them all that the mourning was over, and the king was once again attending to the business of governing (2 Samuel 19:1-8).

The city gate was important in other ancient cultures as well. Esther 2:5-8 records that some of the Persian king's servants plotted at the king's gate to murder him. Mordecai, a leading Jew in Persia, heard the plot and reported it to Esther who gave the news to the king (Esther 2:19-23). The Persian court officials were identified as being 'at the king's gate' (Esther 3:3).

But very importantly, to control or possess the gates of one's enemies was to conquer their city. Part of Abraham's blessing from the Lord was the promise that his descendants would be blessed and that they would possess the cities (or gates) of their enemies (Genesis 22:17). Here Rebekah receives the same blessing, "may your offspring possess the gates of their enemies." Genesis 24:60. And it's this verse that I want to focus on now for it has significance for the Bride in the exercising of her authority.

You will remember the story of Eliezer and his search for a wife for Isaac, recorded in Genesis 24 and how after

Rebekah had accepted the invitation to go with Eliezer, her guardians blessed her with these words. Let's look at this verse again: "Our sister, may you increase to thousands upon thousands; may your offspring possess the gates of their enemies." Genesis 24:60.

We need to ask who are the offspring and what blessing were the guardians decreeing? The offspring are the many thousands and thousands promised now to her, a similar promise to that which Abraham, her father-in-law, had received years previously. This promise refers ultimately to Jesus the Messiah of course, who would not only possess the 'gates of every city' but of all nations and every demonic stronghold. However, historically it also refers to the Israelites and indeed also to us all, who by spiritual adoption have been made part of the covenant promise to Abraham.

I would like to emphasise again that the outworking of the blessing that was bestowed upon Rebekah was simply because of who she was in relation to Isaac. On her own she had no reason to receive the promise and to 'possess the gates' of her enemies on behalf of her descendants. But because of who she was now (the bride) in relation to Isaac her husband, she was able to receive it. Similarly we also can inherit that blessing being the spiritual offspring of Rebekah and more so, since we have King Jesus as our husband, with whom we share authority. However remember that this shared authority as the Bride is not based on our position or title or natural ability but upon our relationship of intimacy with and submission to our Bridegroom, King Jesus, Yeshua Hamashiach.

Sarah, Rebekah and Esther, all types of the Bride of Christ, expressed great humility and submission towards their husbands. Our submission to Christ, as His Bride, the Wife of the Lamb, is that which alone enables us to exercise authority 'at the gate'; to judge and to rule over issues; to decide and to proclaim and decree at the gate on Her husband's behalf but only if she knows the mind of her Bridegroom King. The queen's authority rests upon her intimate dependency on the King rather than on any autonomous role or position.

Paul affirms this when in talking to the Church in Ephesians 5 about marriage relationships when he stresses that wives should be in submission to their husbands and then at the end of the passage says that he is actually talking about Christ and His Church. We as Jesus' Bride can only minister with authority if our relationship with Him is right.

One glorious day in the future after the Marriage of the Lamb, the Bride will become completely 'one with Him' and as His co-partner will reign in great splendour. We only reign because we reign with Him and in Him. It is then that the scripture in Psalm 45:13-14 will be fulfilled for at that point He will have made His Bride to be all glorious: "All glorious is the princess within her chamber; her gown is interwoven with gold. In embroidered garments she is led to the king." Psalm 45:13-14

Chapter 26: The Revelation of the Eternal Nature of the Bride

"Now you are the body of Christ, and each one of you is a part of it." 1 Corinthians 12-27. "Dear friends, now we are children of God, and what we will be has not yet been made known." 1 John 3-2.

These previous chapters share some precious revelations about the Bride but these only paved the way for this revelation about the eternal nature of the Bride; a revelation which has incredible ramifications. The corporate and glorious Bride is not only authorised to intercede in the Heavenly Courts and possess the gates of her enemies because of her dependence upon her Bridegroom, but also because of her eternal nature.

She is able to operate from within time and space AND outside of it. She is also able to bridge both. This is because the Bride occupies an eternal space, from where she operates. I'd like to explain this revelation further but first I want to explain the major differences between the Body of Christ and the Bride of Christ. This will help us to understand and appreciate the awesome uniqueness of the Bride's character and function and the measure of her authority.

The Body of Christ (the Church):

"Now you are the body of Christ, and each one of you is a part of it." 1 Corinthians 12-27. A definition of the Body of Christ is that it is the Church made up of all those who have accepted Jesus Christ as their personal Saviour. They are those "born not of natural descent, nor of human decision, but born of God" John 1-13. The term 'the Body of Christ' describes both its relationship to Jesus as its head and emphasises to whom it belongs. It also describes its functionality in having many diverse parts each with a unique role and gifting. There must be unity and co-ordination within the whole Body, the Church, in order to function cohesively since there is only one Body.

But the Church, the Body of Christ, exists on earth in the first of the two periods of Church history, that is, of the Mortal period of the Church. She exists in a mortal dimension and in an earthly time zone subject to that time and physical space. She exists as the Body of Christ on earth, representing Him here on planet earth. A popular way of emphasising this truth is to say that we are His hands and His feet, so to speak.

A day however will come when she transitions totally into an immortal state and then experiences an eternal existence. At the rapture she will be transformed and perfected and then as His eternal Bride will be fully prepared for the Wedding of the Lamb. At that moment, when she is totally compatible with Her Bridegroom, she will then enter her immortal state.

The Bride of Christ:

At that appointed moment in time, the Church will pass from its mortal state and the mortal period of Church history into the immortal. Scripture says, "In a flash, in the twinkling of an eye, at the last trumpet. For the trumpet will sound, the dead will be raised imperishable, and we will be changed.

For the perishable must be clothed with the imperishable, and the mortal with immortality." 1 Corinthians 15:52-53.

On that day the Church will transition from being the Body of Christ here on earth to the Bride of Christ who, after the Marriage, will return to earth to reign with Him but will do so from a place within both time and eternity. She will be on earth during the Millennium reign but each member will have a resurrected and transformed body just as Jesus did after he was resurrected. He then demonstrated supernatural abilities superior to those he had experienced in his pre-resurrection form and we will too.

In His resurrected form, He was able to suddenly appear in a room to the astonishment of His disciples or then later ascended in bodily form up into the clouds back to His Father. Like Jesus we will be able to move between both the natural and spiritual realms, operating in both dimensions. And because of our resurrected form we will be able to operate from a place both inside and outside of time, and beyond physical space, yet also within the physical realm of time and space.

But what about now? Are we not learning now to embrace our Bridal identity by faith and through the Holy Spirit within us? Are we not learning to walk as His Bride and minister as His Bride even now? Yes, and even though we will not experience until the day of our wedding the full measure of our Bridal authority and anointing, yet we have been betrothed to Him and He to us and that is legally binding. Remember that in Jewish culture a woman is actually considered as a wife as soon as she is engaged and her covenant to her husband has already been registered but then it is ratified at the wedding ceremonies and festivities that take place and is consummated in the bridal chamber.

During her engagement period she enjoys many of the comforts and assurances that her Bridegroom has prepared for her, the attention, support, reassurance, reminders and gifts. These are brought for her, from him, by his 'best man'. During that time she is encouraged to live as set apart, as if already his wife, for she is pledged to him, though separated for a while from him while he prepares their home. Likewise we too, while still awaiting the consummation of our marriage, are pledged to Him. We can whilst waiting begin to embrace our new identity and by faith experience some of its spiritual empowerments. Our Bridegroom sends the Holy Spirit, the 'best man' for us, who helps and encourages us to do this as we prepare ourselves for our wedding.

Of course, during this mortal Church period, the Bride will continue being transformed into His likeness and is not completely compatible with Him yet, but I do believe that even though we are still on earth and found within the Body of Christ and are still awaiting the consummation at that wedding, we can through the help of the Holy Spirit and by faith anticipate that which is to come. We can begin, through that same Spirit and by faith, learn to function as the Bride now and do so from that eternal space.

Though we may know now only a measure of what is the fullness, "for now we see in part and know in part", yet this must not stop us from operating by faith from that spiritual and eternal position. So let me say it once again. We can even now experience what it is to be the Bride of Christ though here still on earth. As part of His body as a result of our new birth we share in His spiritual nature and because we now understand that we are betrothed to Him we can embrace and begin to experience something of what is to become our ultimate identity.

So the question is, how do we experience it?

We do this by simply believing in our hearts that we are the Bride and by confessing it with our lips and then by living it out.

This corporate being, this glorious Bride, that the Father always destined us to be, is created to reflect His great glory just as the moon does the sun. We are endowed with His authority and creative word to both release and to bind, to establish and demolish, to restore and transform and like Esther enter His Courts, stand before His throne and hear Him say, "What is it, Queen Esther? What is your request? Even up to half the kingdom, it will be given to you." Esther 5:3.

So, in conclusion, what are the ramifications of all this? They are numerous and glorious especially for the work of the interceding Bride. Not only do we have His delegated authority but because of our spiritual eternal nature and the place from where we operate, we can by faith go back in time and space to pray into events within mortal history and cancel out any negative consequences or invoked curses.

I was sensing that the Father was sharing with me a profound mystery and He continued to do so in a rather humorous and natural way.

"It's a little bit like your film Back to the Future but not entirely", He said.

This intriguing film is about an inventor who makes a car that can travel back in time in order to rearrange situations in history and cancel out catastrophies and tragedies.

"You too can go back in time", He added. "Not physically or actually as in the film of course but by faith. As believers in My son and as His Bride, you operate in the realm of the Spirit and being, 'seated in heavenly places with Him' can operate in the spiritual dimension outside of natural time and physical space. Therefore you can speak into times past. However, you cannot change the events of history, but you can change by your intercession and your decrees the consequences of history past so they no longer affect history present and history future."

However, I want to stress that carrying out such prophetic activity must be done with such great caution and with a deep sense of 'the fear of the Lord'. This whole ministry area can be so easily abused. Our so called guidance can be based on mere presumption and motivated by enthusiasm. Any prophetic action or any decrees made must be agreed upon through a process of corporate discernment and with the witness of the Holy Spirit.

"It seemed good to us and the Holy Spirit." Acts 15:8.

I sense that today there are far too many 'flaky' prophetic decrees or pronouncements made hastily by sincere believers but which are later proved to be false or have no substance. Great caution and humility is required.

So to summarize, if I have understood correctly, as the Bride we do have the authority to activate change in the present by cancelling out the consequences and curses of events from the past. This enables there to be an alignment between heaven and earth so that His Kingdom comes "on earth as it is in heaven".

As the Bride we can enter the Courts of Heaven and make representation to the Father who is the Judge of all. And we can also decree at the gates here on earth and declare things that are not as if they are because we have I suggest that authority granted to us.

Chapter 27: Exercising Bridal Authority in Intercession and by Proclamation and Decree

The Bride of Christ is created to enjoy much intimacy with her Bridegroom and she is also learning to exercise the authority that Her King has invested in her. However she must always remain in a place of submission and service towards her betrothed. Surely this must be the attitude of all believers and all Christian ministries too.

The Bride must remain postured like the King's maid who stands in the shadows watching his every movement, the wink of his eye, the nod of his head, listening for the change of inflexion in His voice that might indicate something he is about to request.

Psalm 123:2 "As the eyes of servants look to the hand of their master, as the eyes of a maidservant to the hand of her mistress, so our eyes look to the LORD our God." This is her delight. This is her joy. This is her fulfilment. But we are more than just a maid. We are a bride and our King is also our heavenly Bridegroom and He has appointed us to act on His behalf and to exercise great authority in His name. He has chosen to give us Bridal assignments and ministries that are designed to accomplish His will and which will fulfil His prophetic declarations.

As we do this we learn to gain confidence in who we are and in what He expects of His Bride. And though still on earth and still to be perfected, we can even now know something of this now as a foretaste of what it will be like when reigning as fully 'One' with Him in the age to come.

I would like now to share personal testimonies from my own journey which illustrate something of this bridal authority. I do so in order to enable you to grow in that authority yourself but I do it tentatively and humbly because I'm so conscious of how testimonies can be misused to exalt the flesh and do not glorify God alone. My hope is that you will be encouraged by it and indeed, give Him all the glory.

Because the bride operates from an eternal place and spans both time and space, she can, as said in the previous chapter, make declarations and decrees that can affect things in the physical realm in another part of the world, whilst you in your human body, remain physically in your home nation. The proclamations and decrees that you speak out, if made in faith under the anointing and leading of the Holy Spirit, will transverse time and place and will activate changes in the physical realm and atmosphere of the place for which you are praying.

Perhaps the most vivid example of this for me was when I was asked on a phone call late one night just before bed time, to pray for a desperate situation in Pakistan. I had ministered in Pakistan several times before this wonderful miracle happened and had made many friends there. Often Pastors would ring me in England for fellowship or advice or for prayer but this particular night a very distraught pastor with a very urgent request rang me. I could tell that he was very upset.

"Hello Pastor Howard, please, please help us", he cried. "Please pray for a senior Elder of our church here in Lahore. He has been taken into hospital having suffered a heart attack and is not expected to last the night. He is on a life support machine and we have gathered some of his family together to be with him in his last hours. Please pray for a miracle. Only a mighty healing miracle will save him now."

I listened and could sense the anxiety and pain in the Pastor's voice. I quickly agreed that I would pray and began to align myself with the Spirit. I was about to begin to speak when I was arrested in my own spirit and sensed that God wanted the Pastor to assemble not only the Elder's family members but also the church leaders, at the hospital. I told him this and asked if it was possible? He agreed and said he would ring me back when all this had been done. Meanwhile I remained in the Spirit at home and waited.

About 30 minutes later my mobile phone rang and it was the Pastor again assuring me that everyone was present and were now gathered around the hospital bed. I began to remind everyone of the two powerful prayers that Jesus taught about and recorded for us in the New Testament. I sensed that the Lord wanted us to use them in this moment of crisis. The first was found in John's Gospel where we are assured that if we ask anything in the name of Jesus the Father will do it. John 14:13 "And I will do whatever you ask in my name, so that the Father may be glorified in the Son." Then in John 14:14 "You may ask me for anything in my name, and I will do it." And John 16:23 "Very truly I tell you, my Father will give you whatever you ask in my name."

Oh what power there is in the name of Jesus. What authority! So we declared and confessed our faith in that truth, both to ourselves and to one another.

I then shared the second most powerful prayer which was the prayer of agreement. I reminded everyone what Jesus had said in Matthew 19:18 "Again, truly I tell you that if two of you on earth agree about anything they ask for, it will be done for them by my Father in heaven." We encouraged each other to embrace this truth too and to anticipate an answer to our prayer as a result.

So now it was time to intercede and make our requests to the Father based on these things. However I was not really prepared for what happened next and what I found myself praying for. I began to open my mouth hoping to express the thoughts and desires of those gathered. I began by saying, "Father, we come into Your courts at this time to intercede on behalf of our dear Christian brother Your son who is so sick. We ask You to show Your mercy and great favour towards him. We ask You to restore him to full health and not allow anything to rob him of his allotted days.

We declare that whatever Satan has planned to do to shorten his life will not be allowed to affect him. We declare he shall not die but shall live." So far it appeared that there was agreement between us all and in my spirit I was at peace but then suddenly I found myself saying things that I was not expecting to hear. I listened to myself saying, "And Father, I declare as part of Your Bride that our brother will now be surrounded by a battalion of angels, healing angels who will bring Your grace and healing balm to him. Will You, if it pleases You, instruct that battalion of angels to stand around His bed now. Dispatch them please, if it please Your majesty."

And then I heard myself saying, "And he will wake up, open his eyes, see the angels, be completely healed, be filled with the Holy Spirit and speak in tongues, unplug himself from the various machines and go home."

Understandably there was no response from my Pastor friend on the phone in Pakistan. He was I think lost for words and to some degree so was I. But God had I believe spoken and if He had, then there would be a demonstration of healing. Eventually my Pastor friend spoke up and thanked me for my prayers. I asked him to ring me as soon as there was any evidence of a change in the man's health. I said goodnight and ended the call but I didn't need to wait long because after about 30 minutes, around midnight, my mobile phone rang again. It was the Pastor and in the background there were shouts of delight. Apparently everything had happened exactly as I had declared.

It had been very soon after that prayer on the phone that the sick Elder had indeed woken up in the hospital and saw angels around his bed. He then realised that he was totally healed and began unplugging himself from all life support machines much to the delight and astonishment of the family and church leaders. He became filled with the Holy Spirit speaking in tongues and soon after was cleared by the hospital having discharged himself.

This was such a testimony not only to the family and their church but also to the Muslim doctors and nurses in that

Muslim hospital. God certainly got the glory and I love this story particularly because only the Pastor had ever met me when he had attended a meeting that I was speaking at in Pakistan. To everyone else I was just a 'voice on a phone'.

You will notice the participation and presence of angels in this testimony but you will also notice that I was careful not to assume I had permission to instruct or 'command' the angels. I proclaimed prophetically what the angels would do but I asked the Father to instruct and release the angels and didn't command them myself. The Bible does not have a single scripture that states that we can or should do that.

There are some scriptures from which such assumptions might be made and some great men and women of God feel able to make these assumptions. They would quote Psalm 91:11 "For he will command his angels concerning you to guard you in all your ways" suggesting that the angels are created for us and to minister to us and that gives us authority over them. But notice in the Psalm that it's 'He', the Father, that commands the angels. However we would agree to disagree but not allow our different opinions to divide the Body of Christ.

I tend to urge caution in these matters and unless there are clear instructions in scripture regarding what may become a Christian practice, I would not presume it to be permissible Making a practice or a theology based on insufficient biblical evidence can be very dangerous.

Chapter 28: Lest we forget Israel; The Bride is the One New Man

"For He Himself is our peace, who has made the two one and has destroyed the barrier, the dividing wall of hostility, by abolishing in His flesh the law with its commandments and regulations. His purpose was to create in Himself one new man out of the two, thus making peace, and in this one body to reconcile both of them to God through the cross, by which He put to death their hostility." Ephesians 2:14 -16.

"Pray for the peace of Jerusalem: May those who love you be secure." Psalm 122:6.

I want to begin by stating strongly that the Church has never replaced Israel and those from the gentile Church have now been 'grafted as a wild olive' back into Her through the cross. Paul make this clear in Romans chapter 11. The One New Man which is the Bride of Christ is made up of both Jew and Gentile who have put their faith in Jesus as their Saviour and Messiah. The term was created by the Apostle Paul in his attempt to address the issue about equality between Jew and Gentile in the early Church. It is a descriptive term emphasising the equality and 'oneness' of the Bride of Christ which includes both Jew and Gentile but is neither Jewish or Gentile in culture or nature because she is a new creation.

No book better explains this than the book of Ruth in the Old Testament and probably the most famous verse in Ruth is this one: "Where you go I will go, and where you stay I will stay. Your people will be my people and your God my God." (Ruth 1:16). This pledge of love between a young Gentile woman and her Jewish mother-in-law resulted in the restoration of Naomi the Jewess and the redemption of the Gentile Ruth. Because of this some would say that the Book of Ruth is a prophetic picture of the salvation of both the Jews and the Gentiles.

It is however, for many reasons, a beautiful book. It's a story about great loyalty and commitment, of dedication and selflessness and devotion, a compassionate love story but of course traditionally it appears to have been written specifically for the nation Israel so that they could see the lineage of David as coming through Ruth and Boaz. Yet there is even yet a deeper spiritual significance within this story.

Not only does it point out the Davidic lineage as through Boaz but points to the fact that God always intended that the blessing He had covenanted to the Jews (Boaz) would also be offered to the Gentiles (Ruth). It was always to be for both Jew and Gentile since He purposed even then that one day the 'two would become one' in the One New Man. The Messiah would be "a light to lighten the Gentiles AND My people Israel".

This story is about that One New Man too.

Brief Background:

The Book of Ruth's author is never mentioned but it was not written by Ruth. Some Bible scholars believe it was written by Samuel but years before David became king as it refers to a 'former time' so the date may have been around 1010 B.C. and appears to be an account that took place during the time of the judges. It appears to be written specifically for the nation Israel so that they could see the lineage of David as coming through Ruth and Boaz.

Famine and Death:

Elimelech and Naomi are an Israelite influential family from Bethlehem. When famine struck the area, they were forced to migrate to Moab which was a pagan nation and that was when Elimelech which means 'My God is King'. died. His death was very significant, for the death of 'My God is King' was a description of the state of Israel at this time and their experience of God.

It would appear that life for Naomi was not good in Moab either as she names her two sons Mahlon and Chilion which means 'Invalid' and 'Pining' respectively. These two sons married Moabite women, Orpah and Ruth.

But both of Naomi's sons died too so it was only Naomi and her two daughters in law remaining. This was a great misfortune for the family because they had no source of income and unlike Israel, Moab had no such support system for widows and orphans.

Naomi meant 'full or pleasant' but she now calls herself Mara which means 'bitter' and the only thing that Naomi can do is to find one of her kinsmen back home in Israel who might help her. She found Boaz and appealed to his generosity and provision.

Naomi in fact tried to persuade both her daughters-in-law stay behind in Moab and although Orpah did, Ruth said one of the most beautiful statements that the Bible has recorded, "Wherever you go, I will go: and where you lodge, I will lodge: your people shall be my people and your God my God" (Ruth 1:16).

Orpah remained in Moab but things were about to change for Ruth, which means 'friend'. She is about to be greatly blessed

Naomi located Boaz, one of the next of kin of her late husband. Boaz means "my strength" and 'Lord of the Harvest' and after returning Ruth went to the fields belonging to Boaz to glean the fields from what the reapers left.

Boaz saw Ruth in the fields gleaning grain and inquired about who she was (Ruth 2:5). They told Boaz that it was a Moabite woman that came with the widow Naomi from out of Moab. (Ruth 2:6). Boaz made her feel welcome and invited her to stay in the area and ensured that she and Naomi would have more than enough grain to eat (Ruth 2:8-10, 15-18). He then invited her to eat with him and the reapers (Ruth 2:14). He begins to show her great favour and love.

The Kinsman Redeemer:

Naomi suggested that it would be best for Ruth to be redeemed by Boaz and to marry him. He would become her kinsman redeemer. Ruth embraced the customs of her adopted Israel and did as Naomi instructed her.

Notice, it was a Jewess called Naomi who introduced the Gentile Ruth to the Redeemer, her future Bridegroom King. ("a light to lighten the Gentiles"). It was also the Jewish disciples and apostles who first shared the gospel with the Gentiles. It was their Jewish scriptures that brought the Gentiles such revelation. The Gentile believer has so much to be grateful to them for.

So Ruth embraced the Jewish traditions and went and washed herself, anointed herself with perfume, put on her best apparel so that she could lie down at the feet of Boaz and uncover his feet. Then Boaz would understand and then tell her what to do next (Ruth 3:1-6).

When Boaz had finished his evening meal, he lay down and Ruth uncovered his feet and lay next to them and Boaz was startled and asked "Who are you?" Ruth said "I am Ruth your handmaid. Please spread your skirt over your handmaiden, for you are a near kinsman" (Ruth 3:9).

Boaz accepted Ruth graciously and said "Blessed you are of the Lord, my daughter, for you have shown more kindness in the latter end than at the beginning, inasmuch as you didn't follow young men, whether rich or poor." He had heard how she had shown kindness to Naomi, her mother in law.

Interestingly not everyone can be a Kinsman Redeemer. There are five special qualifications:

1. They have to have the legal right to redeem.

2. They have to be willing to redeem.
3. They have to pay the price of redemption.
4. They have to be willing to avenge the enemies of the redeemed or protect the redeemed against any future claims from their adversaries.
5. And there has to be a legal transaction made in the presence of witnesses.

This was so in the case of Boaz. He qualified in all these areas. But this is also so of the Lord Jesus who is our Kinsman Redeemer. When we consider what Jesus accomplished through his life, death and resurrection we see that:

Jesus won the legal right over us by the shedding of His blood.

Jesus is willing to redeem. "The Son of Man, the Good Shepherd lays down His life for the sheep" John 10:11. Scripture makes it clear in Philippians 2 that Jesus humbled Himself willingly and became obedient unto death even the death of the cross"

Jesus paid the redemption price. "You were purchased or redeemed, with the precious blood" 1 Peter 1:18

Jesus has and will continually avenge all our enemies. He is the heavenly advocate and forever pleads our case before the throne.

And finally, the transaction Jesus made for us on the cross was ratified in public and before Satan and witnessed by all of heaven.

Isn't this wonderful? And there are so many more spiritual lessons too that we can glean from the book of Ruth. For example, here are just a few:

- Christians are like Ruth, a Moabite, or specifically, Gentiles but God offers salvation, first to the Jews but also to the Gentiles (Romans 1:16; 2:10).
- Then just as Boaz sought after Ruth, and took a deep interest in her, so God sought us (Ruth 2: 6-14).
- When Ruth bowed down at Boaz' feet as her Lord, so we bow down and submit at Christ's feet (Ruth 2:10) and as Ruth humbled herself before Boaz (Ruth 3:4) we must humble ourselves before Christ (1 Peter 5:6; James 4:10).
- God ensures that we will have all of our needs met like Boaz made sure Ruth would have all that she needed (Ruth 2:7-16). She was allowed to collect even that which Boaz had instructed his men to leave.
- Boaz gave Ruth comfort (Ruth 2:13) just as God comforts us. (2 Corinthians 1).
- Just as we have all of our sins washed away and have the righteousness of Christ imputed to us (2 Corinthians 5:21) so Ruth washed herself and put on her best apparel (Ruth 3:3) representing our white linen mentioned in Revelation 19:9 and our "robes and garments of righteousness".
- Finally, Christians have had their sinfulness covered by Christ's righteousness; Boaz gave Ruth the veil

that she was covered with that had been used by Boaz (Ruth 3:14-15).

Boaz had heard of Ruth's kindness. Ruth who can be seen a 'type' or representation of the Bride of Christ demonstrates so beautifully one of the most endearing characteristics of the Bride, that of grace.

Boaz says, "And now, my daughter, don't fear. I will do to you all that you require, for all the city of my people know that you are a virtuous woman. For it has come to my notice how you have taken care of your mother-in-law. And now it is true that I am your near kinsman." However, then Boaz said "But there is a kinsman nearer than I" (Ruth 3:10-12).

We too as believers had another kinsman to whom we were once legally bound and who because of our own sin and foolishness had gained legal right over us – Satan himself. But our true Kinsman Redeemer paid the price for our ransom and redemption. Jesus by His blood won back the right to own us, to love us, and to cover us with His garments', the corner of His skirt was spread over us too.

Satan is no match for our Jesus. In the story here, when the other kinsman, who had the legal ownership finds out that Ruth and Naomi had no inheritance, he declined to take her as his wife and so she was free to be married to Boaz and so Boaz became her 'kinsman redeemer' (Ruth 4:6).

Boaz then went even further and bought all that Elimelech had and Boaz and Ruth ended up getting married and Ruth and Boaz became part of the royal lineage that would extend down to David and hundreds of years later, the lineage of Jesus Christ. However, perhaps the key reason for this beautiful book being included in the canon of scripture, at least in the mind and heart of the Father, is revealed only towards the end of the story.

May I suggest that the key words here in this story are RECONCILIATION and ONENESS.

Notice that to enter into their full blessing both Naomi (a Jewess) and Ruth (a Gentile) had to return to Bethlehem. Ruth 2:5. Bethlehem means 'House of Bread'.

If this book is about the One New Man then the point made here is that 1) they needed to come to Bethlehem, the House of Bread to find their salvation or their Redeemer. The Bread of Life is Jesus of course who is the "mana that comes down out of heaven". And 2) they both as Jew and Gentile needed to come.

We are living in the time and season when both the Jews and Gentiles are 'returning to Bethlehem' as it were, to the House of Bread. There is a blessing there that awaits them both. Notice that these blessings and the covenant conditions they enjoyed of a Kinsman Redeemer, were first given to Naomi (the Jewess) and then extended toward Ruth (the Gentiles).

Yeshuah Himself was first the Jewish redeemer, "the glory of My people Israel" and then, only then, "a light to lighten the Gentiles". The Gentile Bride can only fully enter her destiny if the Jewish Bride enters hers too for the two are part of the one.

Yes, the book of Ruth is indeed about the restoration of Israel who is represented by Naomi, but its also about reconciling Naomi (Israel) to Boaz (the Messiah, her Kinsman Redeemer). That is, the Jews to their Messiah

It is also about the salvation of the Gentiles for Ruth was a Gentile and about her becoming one with Naomi (the Jewess). It is indeed a parable about the One New Man.

It is also about the Bride, yes, but not just a Gentile Bride nor a Jewish Bride but a 'One New Creation' Bride. She will be an amazing glorious new creation made up of both Jews and Gentiles yet neither Jew or Gentile but a glorious creation at the sight of whom all of nature will marvel and rejoice for it has been, "eagerly awaiting these sons of God to be made manifest" Romans 8:19.

Ruth the Gentile was blessed because she "looked after her Jewish mother-in-law. Ruth the Gentile looked after Naomi and was blessed. And Boaz saw it. The 'Lord of the Harvest' saw it, and blessed them for it!

Jesus too is the Lord of the Harvest. He sees and takes notice when the Gentiles Church begins to serve and care for her Jewish brothers and sisters, prays for them, and serves them. Then the Lord sees it, and blesses.

We must pray for Israel and for Jerusalem and the salvation of His people for God says "I will bless those who bless you (Israel) and curse those who curse you". Because of Ruth's (the Gentile) generosity toward Naomi (the Jewess) God blessed Ruth not only with marriage but with a son. And Ruth not only blessed Naomi but restored her too in a way she could only have dreamed of. Ruth 11:13 tells us that Boaz took Ruth as his wife and she bore Obed which means 'service, usefulness, fulfilment'. Yet the fruit of this relationship also brought restoration for Naomi (Israel)

But how was Naomi blessed by the birth of Obed?

Of course Ruth was blessed as the birth mother and Naomi too by having a new child born into the family, but Naomi was so much more blessed than this. Scripture records in Ruth that all the people said of Naomi on that day, "The Lord has not left you this day. May He (Yeshuah) be to you Naomi (Israel) the restorer of life through Ruth (the Gentiles)".

What did this mean? In what way was Naomi's 'life' restored? Well, Naomi in her old age was able to take Obed and raise him as her own child on Ruth's behalf and even her neighbours (the sons of Ishmael, the Arabs) said, "A child has been born to Naomi".

Isn't it wonderful that through a gentile and through the restoration of Naomi we can see a picture of the restoration of Israel. By the Gentile believers praying for, caring, loving and honouring their Jewish brothers and sisters we will see them coming to Yeshuah as their Messiah. Yet we must also always remember that just as it was Naomi the Jewess that introduced the gentile Ruth to her Kinsman redeemer, so it was the Jews who first brought the gospel to the Gentiles. We need each other. The Bride is incomplete without both.

In the acceptance by the Jews of Yeshuah as the Bread of Life, their Messiah, we will see the number and make-up of the Bride completed. Then the trumpet shall sound, the Lord of the Harvest, our Bridegroom King, will Himself return, the Wedding of the Lamb begin. The consummation of the Bride will take place and 'that woman', hidden in heaven, yet seen in the stars but not made manifest, will be seen by all upon the earth.

Chapter 29: The Call2Come Core Message – Even so, Come Lord Jesus

"He who testifies to these things says, "Yes, I am coming soon." Amen. Come, Lord Jesus. The grace of the Lord Jesus be with God's people. Amen." Revelation 22:20-21.

"The Spirit and the bride say, "Come!" Revelation 22:17. "Let us rejoice and be glad and give Him glory! For the wedding of the lamb has come, and his bride has made herself ready." Revelation 19: 7.

We are living in exciting days. Much of what the Spirit is revealing about the Bride today has been reserved for these times that we are living in, in order to prepare us and invite us to a wedding. Yes, you have a wedding invitation. However this invitation is not just an invitation to attend as an observer or even as one of the bridesmaids or the best man but as the Bride herself.

The journey for both Mike and myself, separately and now together, had taken us on an ascent to climb up towards Him where we could see things from His perspective. God Himself had been drawing us as He does all of His children. And now that we had come closer to the mountain peaks, the focus and mandate of the ministry given to us had become much clearer. This mandate was to announce the coming of the Bridegroom King. It was to awaken and prepare the

Church as Jesus' precious Bride and, like John the Baptist, to make the way smooth.

At the centre of this ministry which we call Call2Come there lies a core message which teaches that we, as believers and as His precious Bride, should cry 'Come Lord Jesus' now and not wait until some future moment when we consider we are better prepared. We believe that when we cry come we will accelerate His coming and bring ourselves more quickly to the point of preparedness for the wedding of the Lamb. This core message is based on the scriptures found in Revelation 22 and in particular on Revelation 22:17: "The Spirit and the Bride say 'Come!'"

Interestingly, this chapter in Revelation is of course the final chapter in the Bible and we believe that it is purposely placed there since it represents the final message that the Spirit of God wants us to hear and that which He is saying to the Churches especially in these end times There is nothing more to be added after this. The Bible narrative closes at this point.

This core message is based around the Greek word 'erchomai' which means 'to come' and is found seven times in this last chapter of the Bible. In fact, the very last few lines of the Bible constitute a prayer by John which includes the word 'erchomai', and is how the Bible ends. It says, "He (Jesus) who testifies to these things says, 'Yes, I am coming soon.'" And John replies, "Amen. Come, Lord Jesus!" Revelation 22:20.

It seems to me that every time this word is used in this chapter it progressively emphasises the developing scope and width of the invitation both to 'come' and to cry 'come'. There is also an increasing intensity and urgency with every appeal or invitation. The whole chapter builds as if towards a climax. It reaches a crescendo with John's final words that seem to be an emotional, spontaneous response from John's heart to Jesus' statement. It seems that John cannot contain himself any longer and almost as if with a sigh he cries, "Even so, Come, Lord Jesus Come!".

We are told in Revelation 19:7 this, "Let us rejoice and be glad and give him glory! For the wedding of the Lamb has come, and his bride has made herself ready. Fine linen, bright and clean, was given her to wear." Although this is a statement, it implies that the wedding will come when the bride has made herself ready. It suggests that the date of the wedding is dependent on her being prepared and when that's so, Jesus will come for it's after this statement in the following chapters that Jesus responds "I am coming soon."

Revelation 22:17 seems to reinforce this when it says, "The Spirit and the Bride say Come!" suggesting that this alignment between Spirit and Bride which is now in place demonstrates the preparedness of the bride. This statement shows that She recognises Jesus in the fullest revelation of His identity as her bridegroom and herself as His bride and therefore is ready for marriage and cries for him to come. She is ready to meet her Bridegroom.

This prayer is a prayer of Bridal love and expresses a deep longing for Him. It is a prayer that only those who long for intimacy with Jesus can pray.

273

So when can She call?

If we are a part of the Bride and hopefully by journeying with us through this book you now know that you are, then this question becomes very personal. We need to answer the question....Can WE cry come, NOW?

We may recognise that cry is even now within our own hearts, deep within our own spirit. We may already long to see him. I find I do and often I hear myself crying "Maranatha, Come Lord Jesus."

But although this may indicate a longing within our own hearts the question still remains – can we pray this prayer today or do we have to wait for some unspecified time in the future to cry 'come,' when we are perhaps more ready than we are at this moment? And how do we know when we are ready?

And if we can cry come now then will this prayer and the cry of "Come Lord Jesus," actually release something in the spiritual realm that will accelerate the Lord's return? And could it be that that cry is itself a demonstration of the fact that we are even now in Father's eyes prepared? I think it does.

The answer lies in the uses of the word Erchomai in Revelation Chapter 22. In Revelation 22:17 after the prayer of the Spirit and the Bride for Jesus to come, it says, "And let him who hears say, 'Come!' whoever is thirsty, let him come; and whoever wishes, let him take the free gift of the water of life." Here we see a clear invitation to those who have ears to hear to say 'Come' and join in this call. If believers will listen to the Holy Spirit within them they will recognise that cry of the Spirit and align themselves with Him and cry, 'Come!'

This is then followed by a further invitation to those that are wanting to drink of the water of life but who as yet have not realised who the 'Living Water' is. Receiving this water and the forgiveness Jesus gives begins the process within of spiritual transformation. We become adopted by the Father as His children and begin to be prepared as Jesus' Bride. This Bridal invitation is for them too, for it is never too late to receive salvation and join the Bridal Company. Yes, we are all called to align ourselves with the Spirit and cry for the Lord Jesus to come!

But sometimes, a false sense of humility or an overwhelming sense of our own unworthiness can cause us to hesitate in accepting our Bridal identity. Somehow we feel we have to qualify or reach a certain level of 'readiness' or 'goodness' before we can accept who He says we are. But if this prohibits us from feeling worthy of calling for Him as His Bride, then likewise we too would never ever have entered into salvation because we would not have then come to Christ until we felt we were 'good enough'.

Hallelujah, it's our hearts response that counts, NOT our own perfection. And as in all things in the spirit realm we first believe in our hearts and then confess with our lips and we then enter in by faith. So it is by accepting 'the water of life' and coming to Jesus and then by accepting our Bridal identity and aligning ourselves with the Spirit to cry 'Come!' that we demonstrate our preparedness.

When we accept who we are as His Bride and cry 'Come' then we activate something that is already within our own hearts. It is the cry within our own hearts for Him. When we pray 'Come,' we align ourselves with the Holy Spirit within us who has always been crying come and this enables Him to complete the work that He has begun in us and accelerate the preparation process. So yes, we can and must pray this prayer now, for it is not only evidence that we are part of His Bride, but also a necessary process in our Bridal preparation itself.

And so, we have a seven-fold sequence about the Lord's coming in Revelation 22:

1. The Lord says that He is coming soon. v 7.
2. The Lord is coming soon and will bring his reward with him. v 12.
3. The Spirit and the Bride say "Come!" v 17.
4. Let him who hears say, "Come!". v 17.
5. Let the one who is thirsty come. v 17.
6. Yes, I am coming soon. v 20.
7. Amen. Come Lord Jesus. v 20.

So, why is He delayed in His coming? If we are encouraged to cry 'Come Lord Jesus' now why has He not yet come. It's because we believe there is something the Father wants to do first. Let me explain.

He is delaying His coming because He is taking us on a journey, a journey of intimacy and longing.

This journey is to a place where nothing else matters but seeing Him. Where nothing else matters than His desire to see us and to take us as His Bride to The Wedding. As we journey, His desire and His longing to receive us becomes our highest concern and our love for Him is what drives us and is all we live for. It's when this desire to see Him reaches such an intensity that it will drive us to call for Him to return and He will come and take us to the Wedding of the Lamb. When nothing else but this will satisfy us, then we will be completely aligned with the Spirit. For nothing else fulfils the heart of Jesus more and satisfies our own.

Song of Songs describes this journey we must make towards that place of deepest longing. Song of Songs 2:16: "My lover is mine and I am his." Notice that although the Shulamite woman is indeed in love with Solomon, she is still preoccupied with herself and the benefits and pleasures of him being hers. Likewise with us, when we begin our relationship with Jesus, our Bridegroom King, we too are preoccupied with our salvation experiences and the blessing that comes as a result. It's more about her own salvation and He is her Saviour, her Redeemer. The *"I am His"* seems like an afterthought.

Then in Song of Songs 6:3, it changes. She now says, "I am my lover's and my lover is mine". The statement is reversed. He being hers becomes the afterthought. Finally in Song of Songs 7:10 she says, "I belong to my lover and his desire is for me." It's all about Him now and His desire. She lives only for Him and is preoccupied with His desires. Now she knows who she is. Her significance is in Him alone. She is His glory. Her beauty is merely a reflection of His Beauty. She truly owes everything to Him and She is His possession.

Her desire is to please Him and His desire has become her preoccupation.

It's at this point that we begin to recognise that the Holy Spirit has taken us on a journey towards someone whom we knew before but somehow who is now appearing differently, who now seems to be showing us that He Himself has another identity. We do know Him as our Saviour but there is more. Yes, it's Jesus still, but He is no longer just the "Lamb of God who takes away the sin of the world." He is no longer just our Saviour.

He is now standing there in the distance waiting for us to follow Him. He's dressed in His Bridegroom apparel with a wedding proposal to make to us and with a wedding invitation in His hand for us. But though this wedding invitation is indeed for you, it is not just for you to attend as a spectator or even as a bridesmaid or the bridegroom's assistant but as His very own precious beloved Bride herself. Yes, we begin to understand. Jesus is also our Bridegroom as well as our Saviour.

This revelation of who Jesus truly is and who we are has been reserved for these end times because Jesus is returning to take us to the Wedding of the Lamb. It's in this season that the Church is receiving this amazing revelation and transitioning in the process.

John the Baptist, as described earlier in this book, had to make this transition in his perception of who Jesus was. He too, from seeing Jesus just as the Saviour, had to move on to seeing Him as the Bridegroom. And we the Church, the

Ekklesia, need to make that same transition. Jesus will always be the Saviour of sinners but His purpose in being incarnate and going to the cross was to firstly redeem mankind and then to pay the dowry price, the purchase price with His blood, for the Bride whom He had come to redeem. He truly is our kinsman- redeemer.

I don't know about you but it seems to me that there are today two very strong 'expectations' of what God is about to do and very soon, in these end times days. One is that He will send a new visitation of the Holy Spirit just before Jesus return which will be like no other revival in history and this will result in what we will recognise as the Great Harvest. It will be a world-wide movement and will sweep across the entire earth bringing many to Christ. Because of this belief many are crying out to God in great anticipation.

And secondly, there is a new movement of God growing ever stronger each day which is to awaken and prepare the Church as His Bride and for Her to call 'Come, Lord Jesus Come!' However I believe that both movements are right and are deeply connected to each other. One is in fact the precipitator of the other. Our loving Heavenly Father does indeed want to send the Holy Spirit again.

He wants to do this 1) to bring that promised revival and see many come into the kingdom. But 2), He wants to do this in order to reawaken and then intensify the love of His Church for Himself so that She can experience the love a bride has for her bridegroom. Then the Bride will have made herself ready and The Wedding will begin.

I want to end this chapter by sharing a vision that Mike received of the Lord because it best describes all that I've just tried to explain. In this vision, the Father and the Son were sitting together in Heaven and they were looking down upon the earth, listening to the many believers praying and calling out to Him to send the Holy Spirit. Their cries were passionate and persistent. They were crying for a revival.

"Do you hear them Father?" the Son said. "They are crying for the Holy Spirit to come. They want You to send a revival. But Father, when will they cry for Me?" Then the scene changed and the Father and Jesus the Son were once again looking down upon earth and were listening to the prayers and receiving the worship of believers. Suddenly Jesus cried out to His Father, "Father, Father. Do you hear them again? Do you hear them? Do you hear what they are crying? They are crying for me to come. Oh Father, can I go now. Please can I go?"

Then the Father looked at the Son and said, "No Son. Not, just yet. But soon though. However, this is one thing we will do. We will send the Holy Spirit just one more time. He will help turn their hearts back to Me and to rediscover the first love for You that they have lost. Then they will long for You and will call for You more. And then, You can go Son, for Your Bride will then have 'Made Herself ready.'

Oh, may that time come soon! May the Holy Spirit bring about that refreshing of His Spirit so that we return to our first love. Amen? Yes, Jesus is our Bridegroom and He is coming back for us soon and He longs to hear us call for Him to Come. So, will you join us in calling for Jesus to Come?

Will you align yourself with the Spirit and cry, "Come Lord Jesus!"

Chapter 30: Preparing Ourselves as His Bride

"Let us rejoice and be glad and give him glory! For the wedding of the Lamb has come, and his bride has made herself ready." Revelation 19:7.

In previous chapters I have tried to show you how it has always been God's eternal plan for Him to give a Bride for Jesus and that one day every member of that Bridal Company would call for Jesus to 'Come!' This cry aligns Her with the Spirit.

However, it is one thing for Father to form a Bride and then to give Her to His Son but how does He manage to perfect Her to be on that day, 'without spot or blemish'? Ephesians 5:27: "to present her to himself as a glorious church without stain or wrinkle or any other blemish, but holy and blameless."

We have also seen in Chapter 27 of this book that although the most effective means of making preparation is to continually cry 'Come' yet our preparation is both a crisis; that which happens in a moment of time, and a process; that which happens over time. The crisis moment is one of revelation when we understand what the Spirit is saying and choose to align ourselves with the Spirit and call 'Come!'

The process is to do with the ongoing renewing and transforming of our minds and hearts so that they eventually align perfectly with His. The Holy Spirit does this in us in two ways: one which is passive and spontaneous as far as the Bride Herself is concerned for it is indeed the work of the Holy Spirit; and the other is that for which she must take some responsibility. Firstly, let's consider what the Holy Spirit Himself does for us so that we can be fully ready and prepared.

In a Jewish wedding the Bridegroom, after their betrothal, must go away to prepare 1) the Chuppah or Huppah, a canopy under which they will get married and 2) the room or Bridal Chamber where they will consummate the wedding, and whilst He is away he sends his 'best man' to take gifts to her and messages of encouragement in case she forgets him. Likewise Jesus our Bridegroom sends the Holy Spirit to be with us while He is away, who reminds us of Himself and "teaches us all things."

We all know that experience of delight when He brings back to our memory something about Him which we had forgotten and which causes us to wonder at His love and care for us. Or He brings a revelation that changes our thinking or action. The revelation that it is right to cry 'Come!' now is one such example. All this is the precious work of the Holy Spirit in conforming us day by day to Jesus our Bridegroom's image and causing us to reflect His beauty.

"But the Counsellor, the Holy Spirit, whom the Father will send in my name, will teach you all things and will remind you of everything I have said to you." John 14:26.

Secondly, there is that active response on our part, in which we fulfil the scripture in Revelation 19:7 where it says, "Let us give him glory! For the wedding of the Lamb has come, and his bride has made herself ready."

Our responsibility is to ensure we are watching with our lamps lit and primed, neither sleeping nor unprepared as were the foolish virgins in Matthew 25. God has provided the 'extra oil' that we need in order to be prepared and despite any attacks of the enemy of our souls and His seemingly long awaited return, we are found alert and ready.

A question many ask us after one of our conferences on 'Bridal Awakening' is, "Please, tell us, how do we prepare ourselves? How do we 'make ourselves ready?'" Generally it is by 'abiding in Him' and earnestly seeking more and more intimacy with Him that the heart is satisfied and the transformation and preparation as the Bride takes place. It's also about breaking through the noise of life into the silence of His Presence, getting away from the many voices in life that scream out and demand our attention.

It's about obeying His invitation to 'come away.' "Arise, my darling, my beautiful one, and come with me." Song of Songs 2:10. We are to come away to a secret place and to sit in His Presence for a while and meditate upon His Word because both His Word and His Presence will transform us and begin to 'make us ready.' So it is written, "By the *word* of your lips I have *kept* myself from the ways of the violent." Psalm 17:4. And, "I have hidden Your word in my heart, that I might not sin against You." Psalm 119:11.

The preparation includes clothes and equipment that we must begin to wear, some of which are our acts of kindness, love and mercy and our acts of supernatural power and miracle (the mighty acts of the Saints as in Psalm 45:14 KJV). And also Revelation 19:7-8 tells us that there are clothes to wear. It says, "Let us rejoice and be glad and give him glory! For the wedding of the lamb has come and his bride has made herself ready. Fine linen, bright and clean, was given to her to wear."

These clothes of fine linen represent the righteous acts: 'righteousness' that is both imputed and imparted and also righteous behaviour and action; and the mighty acts of the saints: works of miracles of healing and deliverance etc. Other garments provided are the 'clothes' of grace and gentleness, forgiveness, and patience and above all humility (the fruit of the Spirit, the nature of Jesus).

We clothe ourselves with the Fruit of the Spirit: Galatians 5:22-23. Then at other times we put on the Armour of Salvation, and so as the Warrior Bride of Ephesians 6 we can be victorious in battle. Dressed in humility and the full armour of God, with the incense of intercession and the perfume of praise, thanksgiving and worship, we will walk in a posture of preparedness and be a constant delight to our coming Bridegroom King.

Another and very powerful way we can prepare ourselves is to begin to reflect on what Scripture says we are to Him, that is to Jesus, and what He thinks and feels about us when He looks at us as His Bride. This will help us to accept and embrace our true end-time identity as the Bride in confidence and assurance and as we do that we will be transformed by the Holy Spirit. What happens is that when we accept what He sees and feels about us then we are agreeing with scripture and believing His Word which cannot lie. To disagree with what He says or feels about us is 'unbelief' and is to make God out to be a liar.

So now I want to look at what Jesus thinks and feels about us, His Bride and I shall do so by looking at just one of the descriptive names or words that the Lord uses to describe us, His precious Bride. I believe that this descriptive name is one of the most significant of all the names that Jesus uses to describe His Bride in the scriptures. It's the word 'dove' and is found in the Song of Solomon. Solomon uses the name of this beautiful bird, the dove, to describe his beloved, the Shulamite woman in the Song of Songs who of course represents Jesus' Bride.

Remember, Jesus, represented by Solomon, first calls His beloved 'My dove,' and then as the relationship between them develops she too addresses him as Her dove. We know that elsewhere in scripture the dove is used to symbolise the Holy Spirit and this gives us a picture of both the power and the presence of God that the Holy Spirit wishes to bring as He comes to indwell. He comes to develop peace and purity, grace and gentleness, sensitivity and humility.

He dove's two wings permanently remind us of the need for balance in our search for truth and in our expression of ministry. It reminds us of what Jesus described as the

Father's understanding of pure worship. Jesus said that the Father seeks those to worship Him in Spirit (supernatural authority and demonstration of power) and in Truth (Scriptural accuracy and integrity of character).

In John 4:23-24 He puts it this way, "Yet a time is coming and has now come, when the true worshipers will worship the Father in spirit and truth, for they are the kind of worshipers the Father seeks. God is spirit, and his worshipers must worship in spirit and in truth." Without both, one wing only, we fly around in the circle of error and imbalance.

However, here in the Song of Solomon the word dove is used for a different reason. It is used in describing the Bride. The Song of Songs has some wonderful things to reveal about you when it describes you as a 'dove': "My dove in the clefts of the rock, in the hiding places on the mountainside, show me your face, let me hear your voice; for your voice is sweet, and your face is lovely." Song of Songs 2:14.

Where will you so often find the dove, the Bride?

The dove makes her nest in the 'high places. The King James text says, "in the secret places of the stairs." Other translations suggest literally, "in the places of going up." This suggests 'to climb higher,' a recognition of a desire within us as the 'dove,' the Bride to reach up, to ascend, and by so doing find Him in a closer and more personal way.

It's a cry for greater 'intimacy'. The Bridal dove longs for intimacy with her Bridegroom. But in order for us to have this fellowship with our Bridegroom, it is necessary for us to get away from it all and ascend into His Presence. It is necessary for us to be in that secret, quiet place away from all the busy turmoil of life, it is, as we've said, to ascend.

Did you know that a dove mourns?

Isaiah 38:14 says, "I cried like a swift or thrush, I moaned like a mourning dove."

Ezekiel 7:16: "All who survive and escape will be in the mountains, moaning like doves of the valleys, each because of his sins."

Yes, doves are peculiar birds, in that they mourn. That for me means that they are very sensitive to the atmosphere and this reflects in their behaviour. I'm reminded of the Beatitude in Matthew 5:4 "Blessed are they that mourn (hunger, thirst, desire, yearn for God) for they shall be comforted". The characteristic of the Bride and of the Bridegroom for His Bride can only be described as an intimate deep yearning for each other, as if in mourning.

Did you know that the dove has special eyes? The dove is a bird that doesn't have peripheral vision. She can see only that which is directly in front of her. The dove, the Bride, only has eyes for that which is directly ahead of her. That is, the object of her gaze; and we too must fix or turn our eyes upon Jesus, 'the author and finisher of our faith.'

Did you know that the dove is without bitterness? The dove does not have a gallbladder you see. That is the part of the bird that is bitter to the taste and must be removed from a chicken for example before being cooked. This means that the dove has no bitterness in her and likewise the Bride is without bitterness. Solomon says to her, "All beautiful you are, my darling; there is no flaw in you." Song of Songs 4:7. And Jesus, our Bridegroom, says that to us too today.

Where will we find the dove? "My dove in the clefts of the rock, in the hiding places on the mountainside, show me your face, let me hear your voice; for your voice is sweet, and your face is lovely." Song of Songs 2:14.

The Dove keeps Herself hidden 'in the cleft of the Rock.' Who is the Rock and what is the cleft of the Rock? Jesus is the Rock and the cleft is our hiding place found in Him. Exodus 33:22: "Then the LORD said (to Moses), "There is a place near Me where you may stand on a rock. When my glory passes by, I will put you in a cleft in the rock and cover you with my hand until I have passed by." Moses experienced this when he hid in the rock and saw the glory of God pass by. The Bride remains abiding in Him for the Dove is "in the hiding places on the mountainside". Just as Moses was hidden so we are hidden in Christ in the cleft and so we the Bride, like the dove, can hide in Him knowing His protection and security.

"Show Me your face, for your voice is sweet and your face is lovely" Oh Bride of Christ; do you know how intense His love for you is? You are so beautiful in His eyes. You may think that you are 'dark' with sin and not worthy of His attention nor His intentions but the truth is you are "dark, yet lovely." Song of Songs 1:5. He loves to gaze upon you for your face is lovely. He loves to hear from you because your voice is sweet to His ear.

Did you know that the dove is a bird of passage? This for me is one of the most beautiful revelations about the Bride. The dove appears in Judea early in the spring when the leaves are coming out, the flowers are opening, and everything looks so fresh and beautiful. This was the time when in the Song of Solomon, Solomon says to her, "Arise, my darling, my beautiful one, and come with me. See! The winter is past; the rains are over and gone. Flowers appear on the earth; the season of singing has come, the cooing of doves is heard in our land." Song of Songs 2:10-12.

The dove remains until the summer is gone and then she flies away to a warmer climate to spend the winter. It is about this that David says, "Oh! that I had wings like a dove! For then would I flee away, and be at rest; lo, then would I wander far off, and remain in the wilderness; I would hasten my escape from the windy storm and tempest." Psalm 55:6-8.

Yes, the dove is a bird of passage, a bird on a journey, and every journey must have a place to journey towards. Likewise as mentioned in previous chapters, every believer is on a journey. We as the Bride are on a journey but our destination is not about a place but a person and our relationship with Him, our Bridegroom. It's a journey about understanding our true identity as His Bride, and Jesus as our Bridegroom King.

So now her preparation as the Bride is nearly complete but there is one more step she must take and one more revelation she must receive. Not only is She to love Him passionately, but from now on She is to understand that Her Bridegroom loves her even more so. And it is that realization that will be so compelling and intoxicating that there will be a total release of her obedience and submission to Him and her adoration of Him.

In the King James Version of Song of Songs 4 : 9, it reads, "You have ravished my heart, my sister, my bride; you have ravished my heart, with one look from your eyes, with one jewel from your necklace." Ravished in this context means to be undone, rendered without any defence or resistance. This is how Jesus feels about us. It is the revelation of the ravished heart of Jesus our Bridegroom for us, that changes everything.

What passion Jesus our Bridegroom has for us! What love! What desire! The New International Version of the bible expresses this verse this way. "You have stolen my heart!" And so it is. (S of S 4 : 9)

As we meditate more and more on our Bridegroom's love for us and grow in the confidence and security that this creates in us, we will become truly prepared for the wedding. Then our dedication to Him and adoration for Him will continue to increase to the point that we will want nothing less than to see Him face to face. We will have no other desire than for Him to come for us. We will find ourselves crying "Come!" along with the Spirit as in Revelation 22:17. We will join in with John the apostle and say "Amen, Come Lord Jesus." Revelation 22:20.

"Maranatha. Come Lord Jesus Come!"

Chapter 31: Understanding this World Pandemic as a Time of Bridal Preparation

"The Sons of Issachar, who (were those in Israel who) understood the times." 1 Chronicles 12: 32.

What is God saying to His Church at this time about this Pandemic and the subsequent lockdowns?

1 Chronicles 12:32 tells us about the 'Sons of Issachar, who were those in Israel who understood the times and seasons.' If ever we needed to be like the Sons of Issachar and understand the time and season we've been going through these past many months it is now. What I want to do in this final chapter is to give you some understanding of what we believe the Lord has been saying to us, as His Church, through this season of Covid 19.

What a time we have had and are still experiencing! It has been a time of much shaking, of change and challenge, of much confusion, and a great deal of fear and uncertainty. However, the positive consequence of the world Covid 19 pandemic and its subsequent national lockdowns has been to cause us in the Church to earnestly seek the Lord for understanding. Many have seen that which has happened as a fulfilment of the words of the prophet Haggai, where God says, "I will once more shake the heavens and the earth." Haggai 2:6.

Many questions have been asked and many voices have been heard, both prophetic voices in the Church and conspiracy theories from the world. In the Prophetic arena, there have been so many conflicting prophetic messages and especially if you widen the scenario to include the last American General Election, where many prophecies about that election and Trump's return to office have now proven to have been wrong. The world's media has been awash with so many theories about Covid, the vaccination and the 'dark elite' and their 'dark agenda.'

We're hearing about the birth of the New World Order, the One World Government, the creation of a New World Economic System, the development of a new form of Humanism which all nations will have to sign up to and the One World Religion. We are told that necessity demands these developments. Populations must be controlled; human behaviour more closely monitored; the use of our world's natural resources more carefully managed and the matter of global warming universally addressed.

And now the development of genetic engineering is being widely sanctioned and with speed. Experimentation with the merging of artificial intelligence with human life is being encouraged. The vaccines and Covid 19 with all its new variants are here to stay and regular vaccinations and boosters will be necessary and become the norm and may even be compulsory if we wish to maintain any degree of independence or freedom of movement.

We are being told that it is a necessary 'world reset' and that the world will never be the same again. We must expect a 'new norm'. Things will never go back to how they were before. This word 'reset' is commonly heard. Politicians, conservationists, and even ordinary people like you and me are saying that this is part of a worldwide reset.

It's been a very difficult time for us all in the Church. Things we always did as Church we couldn't do. programs, courses, and churches closed. So I want here to try to offer some explanation of what we think the Lord is saying to His Church at this time. To put it another way, we want to give an understanding of the Time and the Season we are living in. So, what is the Lord saying to the Church? Like many others, I too set myself to find some answers. An invitation to speak on this subject on an international zoom call coming out of Australia focused my attention and my search.

As I earnestly sought Him I was moved in the Spirit and distinctly heard Him say to me the Hebrew word 'Selah' and then followed it with 'Rest' and then 'Return' and as I mulled over these thoughts I sensed that God was showing me that has been forcing us into a 'Divine Selah'. The word Selah comes 74 times in scripture. It comes 71 times in the Psalms and 3 times in the book of Habakkuk. Its meaning is a little uncertain but most agree it's an instruction to Pause or Rest and Reflect and to Readjust or to Realign before continuing.

I distinctly heard God say, "you need to get My Church's attention. Though the means to get her attention by a Pandemic was not of My making or choosing, I allowed it as a judgment upon the nations. I also perceived it as means of causing a 'Divine Selah,' to all Church activity and Kingdom pursuits. It is My Divine Selah."

As I stayed in the Spirit, Jesus began to share His heart with me. He described the pain that the Church had caused Him. He sighed deeply, "Oh, I am so tired of My people playing at Church as if it were a game to be played, a ritual to go through or a performance to be entertained by. Even worship at times is more concerned about professionalism and its entertainment value than its objective. I do not want firstly your programs and your performances but I want YOU. I want you to experience the delights of My presence and My power. I want you to know My purity and My perfection for I have purposed to share it with you. intimately."

As I sought the Lord over the next few months He turned me to Hosea 2:14: "Therefore, I am now going to allure her; I will lead her into the desert and speak tenderly to her." I understood that this referred to his Church, his Body and that He wanted to draw her into a new place, a deeper relationship with Him, and to reveal her real identity to her. This was her End-Time identity. It was as His Bride. Later He led me back to Song of Songs 2:10: "My lover spoke and said to me, "Arise, my darling, my beautiful one and come with me."

This is when Solomon first expresses his love for his beloved and calls her to follow him. But you will also know that she nervously declines his invitation and when she looks up again he has gone. You will remember how she regrets her rejection of him and goes out searching frantically but he is not to be found. Next time he comes however she is ready and willingly goes with him even to the mountains of myrrh, even though that meant sacrifice and suffering. Their relationship and their romance blossoms to the point at which he is besotted with her you remember, and as I described in the previous chapters says to her in Song of Songs 4:9: "You've stolen my heart, my sister, my bride; you have stolen my heart with one glance of your eyes."

So I believe that this is the season and the time when the Holy Spirit is inviting us to experience a far deeper relationship with the Lord Jesus than we have ever known previously. This is part of our preparation for what is yet to come. We are living in a period of Bridal Preparation and this is another opportunity offered to us.

Then Jesus reminded me of the previous time He had called out to His Church. As far back as 2008, 'the year of new beginnings,' He said, "the Holy Spirit has begun to transition My Church into a new season." He was asking if we would come away, "but many were still too preoccupied with their Church programs and their personal spiritual ambitions to follow. I needed to get your attention once again and quite decisively and so during this Pandemic when Churches have been closed and many ministry pursuits have been postponed, I have been able to do so, for those who are willing to stop and listen to My Spirit."

At that point in our conversation, I became aware that Jesus had stopped speaking and the Holy Spirit was now speaking: "As the moon reflects the sun and has no glory in itself so We want you to radiate and reflect Our glory too. As the moon must position itself to reflect the light so you must position yourself to reflect Ours. And so you need to 'Come away with Me' and follow hard after Me just as the Shulamite woman did.

I want to take you on that journey to somewhere that you have never been before and towards 'Someone' who will capture your heart so deeply that you can never be the same again. The Father has purposed to give you to 'Someone' He loves so dearly. You belonged to the Father first as His sons and daughters but He has always planned to give you to His son as His bride. The question is whether you will go on that journey? It's a journey towards intimacy with your Bridegroom."

As I pondered on this I was reminded once again of that other story in the Old Testament where a similar invitation to 'come away' is given and that's in Genesis 24 where Abraham instructs Eliezer, his chief servant, to go and find a bride for his son Isaac. You remember that here Abraham represents our Heavenly Father, Eliezer, the Holy Spirit; Rebekah, the Bride of Christ and Isaac, the Lord Jesus. And

Eliezer travelled a long journey to Abraham's own people and found Rebekah at the well.

Rebekah was asked to go on a journey to meet her Bridegroom. She was asked by her guardians, "Will you go with this man?" and as God has revealed, the Holy Spirit is searching for a Bride for Jesus today and He is asking you that same question, "Will you go?" Interestingly it was only when Rebekah agreed to go that the servant brought out the Bridal clothes. She stepped into a new identity as the bride when she accepted who she was chosen to become and when she agreed to go on that journey.

This is the Season of the Bride. It is a season when the Holy Spirit is searching for a Bride for Jesus and we do well to understand this season and listen and respond to the invitation He is giving us. This 'Selah' is designed to enable us to realign our hearts with His and rediscover the 'first love' that we may perhaps have lost in the midst of all our busyness and preoccupation. The world may be using the word 'reset' but the Church must use the word 'realignment'.

Reset talks about going back to original settings like a mobile phone can be reset to factory settings. The Church cannot go back to how she was before. She cannot operate the way she did before nor think of herself in the same way as she did before. Too long she has been in Babylon which is the world and eaten the fruits of Babylon. It's time to "Come out of Babylon My people!" and return to Zion. The time is now. The 70 years of captivity are up. We have been called out from the systemic Babylonian Church. Just like the exiles in Babylon could not sing the songs of Zion in Babylon so the Church cannot sing the Song of the Bride in Babylon either.

This Pandemic, and the 'Divine Selah' that it has provided, represents for us in the Church both a serious warning and a righteous judgment, but it also offers us an invitation to journey towards something far better. However, to go somewhere else you first have to leave the place you are in. The earlier exodus from Egypt in the days of Moses was undertaken by all the people, whereas the exodus from Babylon was voluntary and not everyone left. It was a matter of choice. And therein lies the judgment. The Church must go forward and not expect a 'return to normal,' to how it was before the Pandemic. There is a new 'Wineskin' to be discovered for He has New Wine to pour out.

Many will hear what the Spirit is saying and not understand, but the Bride WILL hear and understand and WILL respond. Though she will be a remnant: Gideon's army, she will be a Mighty Warrior Bride. There will be pruning and a separation taking place within His Body like the separation between the five foolish virgins and the five wise. The wise will become gloriously preoccupied with making themselves ready both in number and size (through evangelism) and in maturity (through personal preparation and sanctification).

But the days ahead will become increasingly days of challenge and many will fall away through compromise and fear. Those who accept a compromise will partner with the world and stay behind in Babylon. They will embrace the worldly 'reset' rather than realigning themselves in harmony with the Spirit of God. They will succumb to the deception and the persuasiveness of many enticements but those who 'love not their lives unto death' will prevail. These will be known as the 'overcomers'. Revelation 12:11.

Satan has his own agenda and we see his reset being played in this Pandemic before our eyes. So it is not surprising really that there is an increase in conversations about end times, about globalisation, and moves towards global government. The Bible foretells clearly the establishment of a New World Order and we are moving fast towards that situation. And this is no surprise to God either. Satan initiated his first reset when he tried to usurp all authority in heaven before man was created, and being cast out from there has tried to take complete control of planet earth with another reset.

This first world reset was in the Garden of Eden at the beginning of time when Satan deceived Eve, and Adam gave into temptation. A perfect world became a fallen world and sin entered men's hearts. Things could never be the same after the fall as they were before. And today Satan is still deceiving and recruiting other 'Adams and Eves' to fulfil his purposes. There possibly is a 'dark elite' who have a 'dark agenda' who have been deceived by him. Satan has ALWAYS had a dark agenda. Fallen man has always partnered knowingly or unknowingly with him in his intentions.

The days ahead for the Bride will indeed be challenging. That's why the Church must prepare herself now for what lies ahead. She is in the world, as Jesus said, but not OF it. He warns us, "In this world, you will have trouble. But take heart! I have overcome the world." John 16:33. The Church cannot bury her head in the sand. She is His Bride and must prepare herself for her wedding, the Wedding of the Lamb, which will surely come.

So her lamps must be lit and bright not only for the wedding but for the difficult days that will precede it. This is why the preparation of the Bride is so important today. It underlines that the message of the Bride is the most important message found in Scripture and is the message that the Spirit is bringing to the Churches today.

Conclusion

This book has tried to give an account of our journey of ascent towards the Bridegroom. For both Mike and myself the journey began at the moment of our rebirth. Mike and I, though unknown to each other at the time, began by training on the small foothills when at the age of eight we were both saved and called to be disciples of Jesus. However as you have read, it wasn't until years later that we became fellow-travellers and eventually, mountaineers. Travelling together on missions around the world and sharing what we were seeing and hearing from the Lord about the Bride intensified our desire to see more.

It strengthened our relationship, accelerated our progress and sharpened our focus. With each summit of our climb surmounted, the view from that place enlarged our vision. We began to understand more about the Bridal Paradigm and the more we saw the higher we wanted to climb. That process has never stopped and will not stop until we see Him face to face. But at least now we are learning to 'leap across those mountain tops' with Him: Song of Songs 2:8. But we are also learning that we can only do this as we 'lean upon our beloved,' Song of Songs 8:5, because it really is, "Not by might nor by power, but by my spirit, says the Lord Almighty." Zechariah 4:6.

We stand with Paul when he says, "Brothers, (we) do not consider (ourselves) yet to have taken hold of it. But one thing (we) do: Forgetting what is behind and straining toward what is ahead, (we) press on toward the goal to win the prize for which God has called (us) heavenward in Christ Jesus." Philippians 3:13-14.

A prayer: Lord help us always to lean upon You our Beloved. May You help us to fulfil the mandate that we carry and respect the mantel You have placed upon us. May Your Church be awakened and prepared as Your Bride ready for Your return. May Your people hear the Holy Spirit say to them, "Will you go with this man?" because the answer to that question will surely determine their place as His Bride at Your wedding. Amen.

Maranatha. Come Lord Jesus, Come!

A Message from Co-Director of the Call2Come Ministry – Mike Pike

The journey that Howard so colourfully depicts in this wonderful book is one which I have been privileged to take also. Indeed, there is within every child of God an adventurous heart that longs to explore the spiritual heights it discerns possible in scripture. The challenge we are faced with is whether we will listen to or even hear the voice within us which allures the restless soul to find this ancient pathway and take steps into the land of unknowing. I do not speak of some mystic religion devoid of Christ at its core, but a mysticism that can be traced back so far even before time began.

For there in the shadows before Genesis 1:1, behind the veil of the Divine Will was intentionality which beheld the most glorious of all things possible: Father, Son and Spirit, as three persons, co-equal and co-eternal, yet existing as One, determined another should be included in their "glory of oneness", and so the Bride was conceived in the heart of God before the words were ever spoken, "Let there be light".

This glory of oneness is to be found throughout the Holy Writ and no less than in the hallows of Gethsemane where Jesus prayed that we may be one, not only with each other but also with Himself. This is no trifle sentiment without meaningful form and no empty promise without commitment; instead this Divine Intent has been written into an unbreakable marriage covenant sealed by His own blood of which there is no pulling out, because Jesus and therefore the Godhead have crossed the line of no return.

Hebrews tells us that this incarnate Jesus is the same yesterday, today and forever. As incredible as it sounds, Jesus has forever taken on human form: there is a man in Heaven with a resurrected body, the Lord Jesus Christ! Yet whilst fully man, He has always fully retained His deity and therefore became not only the ultimate demonstration of perfect love but has shown how, through Him, it is possible for God and man to co-exist together as One.

It is this Jesus who awaits for His wife to make herself ready; He is the glorious Bridegroom King who will soon return to planet Earth for His bride and take her to the wedding ceremony when all the hosts of Heaven shall sing Alleluia. Then the Eternal Purpose of God conceived before time began shall finally be realised. O what a glorious day that shall be, I can almost hear the growing commotion in Heaven as the final arrangements are being made, place settings and reservations checked and last minute invitations sent out.

This Eternal Purpose of God has set the entire context for creation and all of human history right up to the present day. This Divine Intent creates a present and persistent rhythm which beats in perfect time and to which all spheres seen and unseen must ultimately yield like a great theatrical narrative that builds towards the final scene, and though it is invisible it is no less real. There is a clock counting down to this ultimate climax.

Those who have had ears to hear what the Spirit is saying to the churches, have been quickened by this bridal rhythm and resonated with its message, they have caught a glimpse of the Bridegroom and a profound love has been stirred deep within that cannot be easily quenched. It is this rhythm like a love song from Heaven that Howard and I have both heard individually and corporately together, and our lives have been set on a journey towards the Bridegroom ever since. From 2009 it has been my greatest honour and privilege to partner with Howard having a shared passion to awaken the Bride and help her to get dressed.

Howard has shared his journey to date in this book with his unique combination of storytelling, humour, wisdom and passion. I have loved this about him, and often found these gifts to be of great comfort in the gruelling frontlines of mission around the world. So thank you Howard for the years of friendship and ministry together, as we have laboured as best we could to champion this most holy and glorious of assignments. May the Lord grant us the grace to continue this royal commission even more as we see the Day of the Lord approaching.

For those hungry to learn more about the Bride and what scripture teaches about the days ahead from a bridal perspective then Howard wanted me to introduce here the release of my book. It is a compilation of sixty biblical studies which explore the bridal paradigm in depth and has come from many years of intimacy, study and most of all listening at the Bridegroom's feet through meditation and devotion to Him.

One thing I have learnt over the many years in carrying this message is the necessity for the Bride to be equipped and taught the Word from a bridal perspective. Indeed from Genesis to Revelation, the Bride is there to be found for those who know how to look, and once you see you cannot un-see. It is as though she has much to reveal to the discerning believer. So I wanted to give her a voice that we could hear what she has to say, and that's why the Lord put it on my heart to call it "The Gospel According to the Bride".

About Call2Come

Call2Come is a growing movement around the world primarily focussed on the Second Coming of Jesus Christ and the implications of this 'blessed hope' for the church today. Our mandate is to help the Bride get ready. This preparation is both inward and individual for each believer to grow in their love and intimacy with Jesus Christ, but also outward and corporate.

Our vision: In regions and nations around the world, the Bride of Christ will gather together in times of worship and prayer, to pour out her heart in purity of longing, repentance and proclamation, and ask Jesus to Come.

What We Believe:

1. The Bride of Christ has an urgent mandate that only she can fulfil: to make a way for her Bridegroom King, by preparing a highway of holiness for His return, straight paths of righteousness upon which the King of Kings will return.

2. The Bride of Christ must fulfil her mandate and calling before the great day of the Lord. There is work that only she can do, and prayers that only she can pray.

3. The Bride of Christ is a warrior bride! She stands in the nations of the world as a royal princess and wields in her hand the sceptre of the King. She is His glory upon the earth and is so breathtakingly

beautiful she has many enemies, intent on her demise. But she is not weak, she is very strong. For she is in Christ, and the corporate expression of oneness in the church.

4. The Bride of Christ is planted in the land to effect national transformation and healing. She is an intercessor, the One 'called by His Name' to pray for the healing of nations. 2 Chronicles 7:14.

5. The Bride of Christ has each anointing of the five-fold office. She is an apostle, a prophet, an evangelist, a pastor and a teacher, because she is just like Jesus who was all of these and more, and therefore the Bride is the perfectly complete and compatible 'wife of the Lamb'.

6. We believe there is an outpouring of the Holy Spirit that the church has not yet experienced, in fact it is one that is reserved only for the Bride. It will not be released by asking for another outpouring or revival but is sent by the Bridegroom King in advance of His coming, to help the Bride of Christ get ready when she begins to call upon Him to come.

Find Out More

If you've enjoyed this book and would like to find out more, then there are a lot of resources available for further study and encouragement and also a large online community to connect with.

www.call2come.org

www.youtube.com/c/call2come

www.facebook.com/groups/call2come

Printed by Amazon Italia Logistica S.r.l.
Torrazza Piemonte (TO), Italy

43764098R00174